Thank you for purchasing this book. Your feedback is important to us. After your feedback, kindly send us an email to asiamabertusa128@gmail.com for our free gift

ACKNOWLEDGEMENT

This book is carefully designed to meet the needs of pharmacy technicians of this millennium. It saves time and energy since it focuses straight on the exam knowledge domains. The author's enthusiasm in pharmacy enables him to write this book for anyone who is interested in taking the PTCE. It covers all exam knowledge domains you need to study for and pass your PTCB without writing again and again.

REVISION GUIDE MADE SIMPLE FOR PHARMACY TECHNICIANS

Covers all Pharmacy Technician Certification Board (PTCB) Exam knowledge domains

Simplified notes on each topic

Covers over 270 practice questions and answers

Table of Contents

Chapter 1
INTRODUCTION TO PHARMACOLOGY

PHARMACOLOGY - the study of drugs, their uses and how they affect the body.

There are two main branches of pharmacology:

Pharmacodynamics - how drugs affect the body.

Pharmacokinetics - what happens to a drug when it is administered.

The components of pharmacokinetics:

Absorption -the process where by a drug gets absorbed into the blood stream

The absorption rate affects the bioavailability of a drug.

Bioavailability is the rate and how much a drug reaches

its targeted place of action.

Factors that affect absorption:

Chemical properties

Physical properties

The person taking the drug

Distribution - where drug goes or circulates in the body

Factors that affect distribution of a drug

Tissue binding

Blood perfusion

Cell membrane permeability

Metabolism - a drug broken down by the liver

Factors that affect metabolism

Diet

Age

Sex

Hormones

Pregnancy

Disease

Excretion - elimination of waste from the body

Factors that affect excretion

Biological factors such as age and sex

Drug interaction

Urine flow rate

Distribution and binding characteristics of a drug

How to identify some of the Generic and their Brand names:

Some of the generic drugs have the same alphabet(s) at the beginning of their names as their brand names however, most of them have more than one brand name. The brand name is selected by the manufacturer or the distributor. A drug has at least 3 names; chemical, generic and brand name. The chemical name is not generally offered to study because of its complexity.

List of commonly used drugs (Top 200 drugs)

Generic name	Brand name	Drug class/DEA SCH.
Amoxicillin	Trimox, Amoxil	Antibiotic
Hydrochlorothiazide	HCTZ	Diuretic
Promethazine	Phenergan	Antihistamine
Fluticasone	Flonase	Allergy
Meloxicam	Mobic	NSAID
Citalopram	Celexa	Antidepressant
Aripiprazole	Abilify	Antipsychotic
Methylprednisolone	Medrol	Corticosteroid
Carvedilol	Coreg	C.H.F
Oxycodone	Oxycontin	Pain reliever, Sch.2
Folic Acid	Folvite	Supplement
Pantoprazole	Protonix	GERD/Ulcers

Paroxetine	Paxil	Antidepressant
Pravastatin	Pravachol	High cholesterol treatment
Levofloxacin	Levaquin	Antibiotic
Celecoxib	Celebrex	NSAID
Ciprofloxacin	Cipro	Antibiotic
Penicillin	Pen VK	Antibiotic
Dexlansoprazole	Dexilant	GERD Treatment
Topiramate	Topamax	Antiepileptic
Valacyclovir	Valtrex	Herpes
Clindamycin	Cleocin	Antibiotic
Glipizide	Glucotrol	Treat Diabetes 2
Ropinirole	Requip	Treat Parkinson's
Risperidone	Risperdal	Antipsychotic
Buspirone	Buspar	Anti-anxiety
Minocycline	Minocin	Antibiotic
Phenazopyridine	Pyridium	UTI
Clobetasol	Clovate, Clobex	Corticosteroid
Divalproex	Depakote	Antiepileptic
Simvastatin	Zocor	Cholesterol
Nitroglycerine	Nitrostat	Angina
Cefuroxine	Ceftin	Antibiotic
Travoprost	Travatan	HBP
Lurasidone	Latuda	Antipsychotic

Verapamil	Veleran	Calcium Channel Blocker
Estradiol	Estrace	Menopause
Lisinopril	Prinivil, Zestril	ACE Inhibitor
Metoprolol	Lopressor	Beta Blocker
Nystatin	Mycostatin	Antifungal
Baclofen	Gablofen	Muscle Relaxer
Digoxin	Lanoxin	Arrythmia
Gabapentin	Neurontin	Anticonvulsant
Quinapril	Accupril	Antihypertensive
Aspirin	Bayer, Ecotrin	Pain reliever
Meperidine	Demerol	Narcotic Analgesic, Sch.2
Azithromycin	Zmax, Zithromax	Antibiotic
Ranitidine	Zantac	Antacid/Anti-ulcer
Zolpidem	Ambien	Anti-anxiety. Sch.4
Quetiapine	Seroquel	Antipsychotic
Tiotropium	Spiriva	Anticholinergic
Diclofenac	Voltaren, Zorvolex	NSAID
Enalapril	Vasotec	ACE Inhibitor
Pregabalin	Lyrica	Anticonvulsant
Ezetimibe	Zetia	Antihyperlipidemic
Lisdexamfetamine	Vyvanse	ADHD Anesthetic,

		Sch.2
Tizanidine	Zanaflex	Muscle Relaxer
Morphine	Ms contin	Pain reliever (Narcotic) Sch.2
Nifedine	Procardia	Antihypertensive
Famotidine	Pepcid	Antacid/Anti-ulcer
Sumatriptan	Imitrex	Antimigraine
Lansoprazole	Prevacid	Antacid/Anti-ulcer
Hydrocodone/APAP	Vicodin	Analgesic, Sch.2
Dexmethylphenidate	Focalin	Stimulant/ADHD, sch.2
Escitalopram	Lexapro	Antidepressant
Albuterol	Proair HFA	Asthma
Metformin	Glucophage	Anti-diabetic
Sertraline	Zoloft	Antidepressant
Ibuprofen	Advil, Motrin	NSAID
Cephalexin	Keflex	Antibiotic
Potassium	K-tab	Electrolyte
Benazepril	Lotensin	Antihypertensive
Budesonide	Pulmicort	Asthma
Clonazepam	Klonopin	Anti-anxiety, sch.4
Cyclobenzaprine	Flexeril	Muscle Relaxer
Diazepam	Valium	Anti-anxiety, sch.4
Alendronate	Fosamax	Osteoporosis
Risedronate	Actonel	Osteoporosis
Carisoprodol	Soma	Muscle Relaxer, sch.4

Fluoxetine	Prozac	Antidepressant
Lovastatin	Mevacor	Cholesterol
Rivaroxaban	Xarelto	Anticoagulant
Codeine/APAP*	Tylenol *	Pain reliever *
Pramipexole Dihydrochloride	Mirapex	Anti-Parkinson's
Olanzapine	Zyprexa	Antipsychotic
Diltiazem	Cardizem	Antihypertensive
Glyburide	Diabeta	Anti-diabetic
Cefdinir	Omnicef	Antibiotic
Guaifenesin	Robitussin	Expectorant
Eszopiclone	Lunesta	Insomnia, sch.4
Anastrozole	Arimidex	Treat breast cancer
Cetirizine	Zyrtec	Antihistamine
Esomeprazole	Nexium	Antacid/Anti-ulcer
Vitamin D	Caltrate	Supplement
Metronidazole	Flagyl	Antimicrobial
Testosterone	Androgel	Low Testosterone, sch.3
Enoxaparin	Lovenox	Anticoagulant (blood thinner)
Olopatadine	Patanol	Antihistamine
Fentanyl	Duragesic	Analgesic, sch.2
Tramadol	Ultram	Analgesic, sch.4
Warfarin	Coumadin	Anticoagulant
Loperamide	Imodium	Anti-diarrhea

Oxycodone/APAP	Percocet	Analgesic/Pain reliever, sch.2
Methylphenidate	Concerta	ADHD Antimicrobial, sch.2
Losartan + HCTZ	Hyzaar	Antihypertensive
Triamterene + HCTZ	Dyazide	Antihypertensive
Budesonide + Formoterol	Symbicort	Asthma
Tolterodine	Detrol	Urinary Anti-spasmodic
Amoxicillin/Clavulanate	Augmentin	Antibiotic
Bupropion	Welbutrin	Antidepressant
Omeprazole	Prilosec	Antacid/Anti-ulcer
Hydrochloroquine	Plaquenil	Immunosuppressive /Anti-parasite
Metoclopramide	Reglan	GERD
Meclizine	Dramamine	Antiemetic
Levetiracetam	Keppra	Anticonvulsant
Dicyclomine	Bentyl	Anti-spasmodic
Liothyronine	Cytomel	Hypothyroidism
Levalbuterol	Xopenex	Bronchospasm
Ondansetron	Zofran	Antiemetic
Insulin Lispro	Humalog	Rapid-acting insulin
Dabigatran	Pradaxa	Anticoagulant
Febuxostat	Uloric	Anti-gout
Etanercept	Enbrel	Anti-arthritis
Nebivolol	Bystolic	Beta blocker

Nabumetone	Relafen	NSAID
Temazepam	Restoril	Sleep aid
Triamcinolone	Kenalog	Corticosteroid
Rivastigmine	Exelon	Anti-dementia
Terazosin	Hytrin	Antihypertensive/BPH
Atenolol	Tenormin	Beta blocker /Antihypertensive
Benztropine	Cogentin	Anti-Parkinson's
Mupirocin	Bactroban	Antibacterial
Adalimumab	Humira	Anti-inflammatory
Ezetimibe + Simvastatin	Vytorin	Cholesterol
Naproxen	Aleve	Pain reliever
Cyclosporine	Restasis	Immunosuppressant
Amphetamine/Dextro-amphetamine	Adderall	ADHD/Narcolepsy, sch.2
Ticagrelor	Brilinta	Heart disease
Prednisolone	Orapred	Glucocorticoid
Duloxetine	Cymbalta	Antidepressant
Venlafaxine	Effexor	Antidepressant
Atorvastatin	Lipitor	Cholesterol
Fexofenadine	Allegra	Antihistamine
Vitamin A	Retinol	Supplement
Pioglitazone	Actos	Anti-diabetic
Solifenacin	Vesicare	Overactive bladder
Amitriptyline	Elavil	Antidepressant

Sildenafil	Viagra	Erectile dysfunction
Pregabalin	Lyrica	Anticonvulsant
Estrogen	Premarin	Replacement hormone
Isosorbide mononitrate	Imdur	Cardiovascular(Angina)
Glimepiride	Amaryl	Anti-diabetic
Oseltamivir	Tamiflu	Antiviral
Roflumilast	Daliresp	Anti-inflammatory
Tadalafil	Cialis	Erectile dysfunction
Phentermine	Adipex	Weight loss, sch.4
Hydroxyzine	Vistaril	Antihistamine/Allergy
Mirtazapine	Remeron	Antidepressant
Sitagliptin	Januvia	Anti-diabetic
Propranolol	Inderal	Antihypertensive
Niacin	Niaspan	Antihyperlipidemic
Doxazosin	Cardura	Antihypertensive
Methotrexate	Rheumatrex, Trexall	Anti-rheumatic
Rabeprazole	Aciphex	Antacid/Anti-ulcer
Finasteride	Proscar	Urinary tract agent
Insulin Aspart	Novolog	Rapid acting insulin
Bisoprolol	Zebeta	Antihypertensive
Famciclovir	Famvir	Antiviral
Clarithromycin	Biaxin	Antibiotic
Lidocaine	Lidoderm	Anesthetic
Vardenafil	Levitra	Erectile dysfunction

Ketoconazole	Nizoral	Antifungal
Moxifloxacin	Avelox	Antibiotic
Nortriptyline	Pamelor	Antidepressant
Hydralazine	Apresoline	Antihypertensive
Atomoxetine	Strattera	ADHD Antipsychotic
Varenicline	Chantix	Smoking cessation
Methadone	Methadose	Anti-addictive, sch.2
Ibandronate	Boniva	Osteoporosis
Montelukast	Singulair	Asthma
Lamotrigine	Lamictal	Antiepileptic
Carbamazepine	Carbatrol	Antiepileptic
Insulin Detemir	Levemir	Long acting insulin
Oxybutynin	Oxytrol	Urinary tract agent
Doxycycline	Doryx	Antibiotic(tetracycline)
Levothyroxine	Synthroid	Thyroid hormone
Ramipril	Altace	Antihypertensive
Olmesartan	Benicar	A2RB
Lisinopril/HCTZ	Zestoretic, Prinzide	Hypertension
Hydrocortisone	Acticort, Colocort, Cortef	Steroid
Nitrofurantoin	Furalan	Antimicrobial
Chlorthalidone	Hygroton, Thalitone	Anti-diuretic
Allopurinol	Zyloprim	Antigout

Lithium	Lithonate	Electrolyte
Oxcarbazepine	Oxtellar XR	Antiepileptic
Benzonatate	Tessalon	Antitussive
Timolol	Istalol	Beta blocker
Docusate	Colace	Laxative

Drug-drug interaction.

Warfarin and Aspirin.

Clonidine and Propranolol.

Digoxin and Quinidine.

Potassium Chloride and Spironolactone.

Fluoxetine and Phenelzine.

Food-drug interactions

Grapefruit juice interacts with so many drugs

For example: Grapefruit with statins and antihistamines

Warfarin and green leafy vegetables

Black licorice and Digoxin

Salt and antihistamines drugs

Herbal-drug interaction

Ginseng and Aspirin, Clopidogrel, Diclofenac, Heparin

Garlic and Aspirin

Green tea and Pseudoephedrine

St. John's wort and antidepressants medications

Regular blood test and follow up medications

Digoxin (heart drugs)

Warfarin (blood thinners)

Insulin [diabetic drugs]

Phenytoin [seizure drugs]

Carbamazepine (Seizure)

ACE INHIBITORS [Angiotensin-Converting Enzyme]

Are a category of drugs that block the conversion of angiotensin I to angiotensin II

ACE Inhibitors [generic drugs] end with **PRIL**.

EXAMPLES:

Generic	Brand
Lisinopril	Zestril Prinivil
Enalapril	Vasotec
Quinapril	Accupril
Ramipril	Altace

USES: FOR HIGH BLOOD PRESSURE [HYPERTENSION] and other heart related diseases.

BETA BLOCKERS

Beta blockers are a class of medications used to block the effects of the hormone epinephrine, also known as adrenaline.

Beta Blockers [generic drugs] end with **OLOL**

Examples:

Generic	Brand
Bisoprolol	Zebeta
Nebivolol	Bystolic
Propranolol	Inderal XL
Metoprolol	Lopressor Toprol XL

USES: FOR HBP, ANGINA, ARRHYTHMIA, MIGRAINE, CHF

Proton Pump Inhibitors:

Are a type of drugs that reduce the production of acid by blocking the enzyme in the wall of the stomach that produces acid.

PPI [generic] ends with **PRAZOLE**

Examples:

Generic	Brand
Omeprazole	Prilosec Zegerid
Esomeprazole	Nexium
Lansoprazole	Prevacid
Dexlansoprazole	Dexilant

Note: Aripiprazole is an Antipsychotic drug.

<u>Uses</u>: GERD (gastroesophageal reflux disease)/heartburn.

PPIs reduce the production of acid in the stomach.

CALCIUM CHANNEL BLOCKERS.

Are a class of drugs that relax the blood vessels and increase the flow of blood and oxygen to the heart while also minimizing the work load of the heart.

Calcium channel blockers end with **DIPINE**.

Examples:

Generic	Brand
Amlodipine	Norvasc
Felodipine	Plendil
Nicardipine	Cardene IV
Nisoldipine	Sular

Note: Verapamil, Bepridil and Diltiazem are also Calcium Channel Blockers

USES: FOR HYPERTENSION, ANGINA, MIGRAINE, ARRHYTHMIA.

Cholesterol drugs are drugs used to treat hypercholesterolemia.

<u>Cholesterol</u> [generic]drugs end with **STATIN**

Examples:

Generic	Brand
Simvastatin	Zocor
Atorvastatin	Lipitor
Lovastatin	Mevacor
Pravastatin	Pravachol

Statins drugs work effectively when taken at night.

HISTAMINE 2 BLOCKERS

Are a class of drugs that block the action of histamine at the histamine H2 receptors of the parietal cells in the stomach that results in reducing the production of acid in the stomach.

H2 Blockers [generic drugs] end with **TIDINE**

Examples:

Generic	Brand
Famotidine	Pepcid
Ranitidine	Zantac
Nizatidine	Axid
Cimetidine	Acid reducer Tagamet HB

USES: G.E.R.D, heartburn

HISTAMINE 1 BLOCKERS

Are drugs used to suppress histamine-mediated effects in anaphylactic or anaphylactoid reactions. [Allergic reactions]

Benadryl

Chlor-Trimeton

Claritin

Atarax

USES: For allergic reactions

ANXIETY(Benzodiazepines) [generic drugs] end with **LAM/ZEPAM**

Examples:

Generic	Brand
Diazepam	Valium
Clonazepam	Klonopin
Alprazolam	Xanax

Note: Temazepam is a sleep aid.

USES: For anxiety.

A2R BLOCKERS [Angiotensin II Receptor Blockers]

Are drugs that block the activation of AT1 receptors, thus preventing the binding of angiotensin II.

A2R blockers [generic drugs] end with **SARTAN**

EXAMPLES:

Generic	Brand
Valsartan	Diovan
Telmisartan	Micardis
Losartan	Cozaar
Irbesartan	Avapro

USES: FOR HIGH BLOOD PRE SSURE, KIDNEY FAILURE, HEART FAILURE

HYPERTHYROID DRUGS

Are a class of drugs used to treat overactive thyroid gland.

Methimazole (Tapazole)

Propylthiouracil.

HYPOTHYROID DRUGS

Are drugs used for the treatment of underactive thyroid gland.

Levothyroxine.

Liothyronine

Teratogenic drugs

Teratogenic drugs are drugs that cause abnormality of the fetus (birth defects)

Some of the drugs are:

Thalidomide

Isotretinoin

Alcohol

Cocaine

Lithium

Vitamin A overdose

ACE Inhibitors

Drug class	Side effects
Estrogens	Carcinogenic effect, vomiting, heavy menstrual bleeding, bloating/stomach cramps, vaginal itching/discharge, breast pain
Anticholinergic	Confusion, blurred vision, dental problems, hyperpyrexia, sore throat
Benzodiazepines Nonbenzodiazepines	Drowsiness, headache, memory impairment, irritability, aggression
Androgens	Cardiac problems, diarrhea, redness, acne, stomach pain, hair loss
Penicillin	Fever, joint pain, shortness of breath, thrush, stomach pain, vaginal discharge/itching, headache, diarrhea
Macrolides	Allergic reaction, nausea, diarrhea, vomiting, tinnitus (buzzing in the ear), inflammation of bile duct
ACE Inhibitors	Dizziness, loss of taste, hyperkalemia (increased blood potassium level), Weakness, dry cough, headache
STATIN DRUGS	Drowsiness, vomiting, nausea, abdominal pain, headache, muscle aches, difficulty sleeping, rashes

Note: side effects range from common/mild to severe.

PHARMACY ABBREVIATIONS

Pharmacy abbreviations are also known as sig codes.

PRN	As needed
AC	Before meal
PC	After meal
NR	No refill
HS	At bedtime
PO	By mouth
TIQ	3 times daily
BID	2 times daily
QD	Everyday
PV	Vaginally
PR	Rectally
OU	Both eyes
OD	Right eye
OS	Left eye
AD	Right ear
QID	4 times daily
AS	Left ear
AU	Both ear
IV	Intravenous
ID	Intradermal
IM	Intramuscular
IN	Intranasal
INJ	Injection
Q	Every
Q12	Every 12 hours
SIG	Write/label
Rx	Prescription
QW	Every week
SL	Sublingual
SC	Subcutaneous
SOS	Shortness of breath
STAT	As soon as possible/ Immediately
DAW	Dispense as written
QHS	Every bedtime
NS	Normal saline
DSW	Dextrose 5 in Water
R	Rub
ATC	Around the clock

STRENGH, DOSE, DOSAGE FORM AND ROUTES OF ADMINISTRATION

Strength - Amount of drug in dosage form e.g. 350mg capsule

Dose - Quantity to be administered at one time or specified period e.g twice daily

Dosage form - Physical form of dose of drug e.g. tablet, cream, capsule, ointment

Route of administration - Way dosage form is given e.g. oral, topical, nasal, sublingual

Enteral route - Via the mouth or the anus e.g. oral ,sublingual, rectal, buccal

Parenteral route - Via the vein or skin e.g. intradermal, intravenous, intramuscular

Chapter 2

PHARMACEUTICAL CALCULATIONS

Roman numerals

Ss	½
I	1
IV	4
V	5
IX	9
X	10
XIX	19
XXIX	29
XL	40
L	50
C	100
D	500
M	1000

This sentence below can help you memorize **LCDM**

Luke Can Do Math 5151

Luke for L 50

Can for C 100

Do for   D 500

Math for M 1000

Most commonly used conversions system

1kg	2.2Lb
1gm	15gr
1oz	30gm
1Lb	454gm
1tsp	5ml
1tbsp	15ml
1oz	30ml
1pint	480ml
1gallon	3840ml
1gr	65ml
1cc	1ml
1qt	2pint
1Lb	16oz
1oz	2tbsp
1pint	2cups
1mg	1000mcg
1gm	1000mg
1kg	1000gm
1L	1000ml
1dram	1.77gm

To change Kg to gm to mg to mcg ......multiply by 1000

To change mcg to mg to gm to kg ......divide by 1000

To change hours to minutes.....multiply by 60

To change minutes to hours.....divide by 60

DAY SUPPLY

Day supply = quantity dispensed ÷ quantity taken each day.

EYE/EAR DROPS DAY SUPPLY

Example: Calculate day supply of Loteprednol 0.5%, one drop into each eye 4 times daily. # 10ml bottle.

1 drop × 2 eyes × 4 times daily = 8 drops

(1ml. = 20 drops)

10ml × 20 drops = 200 drops

200 drops ÷ 8 drops = 25 days.

TABLETS/CAPSULES DAY SUPPLY

Example: 1. What is the day supply of Acetaminophen 325mg to be taken 2 tablets 3 times daily by mouth? # 30

2 tablets × 3 times daily

= 6 tablets

30/6

= 5 days

Example: 2. Calculate a day supply of Advil 200mg to be taken 1 tab q6 hours daily # 60.

24 hours in a day. Therefore

24 ÷ 6 hours = 4 times in every 6 hours.

1 tab × 4 times in every 6 hours = 4

60 ÷ 4 = 15 days.

LIQUIDS

Example: 1. Take Robitussin syrup 2 teaspoon q 6 hours PRN for cough # 4oz. Calculate the day supply.

4 times in every 6 hours. (24 ÷ 6)

2 tsp × 4 = 8

(1oz = 30ml)

change 4oz to milliliter

4oz = 120ml

120 ÷ 8 = 15 days

Example: 2. What is the total day supply of an oral suspension of Amoxicillin 125mg/5ml to be taken 500mg b.i.d? # 118ml

125mg/5ml = 500mg/X

Cross multiply to solve for X

125X = 5 x 500

125X = 2500

Divide both sides by 125

X = 20

20 × 2(b.i.d) = 40

118ml ÷ 40 = 2.95

3 days

Example: 3. What's the day's supply for this prescription: Drug B 65mg/tsp, 45mg po every 12 hours? # 84ml

I tsp = 5ml

65mg/5ml = 45mg/X

Cross multiply to solve for X

65X = 45 x 5

65X = 225

Divide both sides by 65

X = 3.46

24 ÷ 12 = 2 times every 12 hours

2 × 3.46 = 6.92

84 ÷ 6.92

= 12 days

Oral Inhalation

Example: Calculate the total day supply of Fluticasone 44mcg, one inhalation 3 times daily, # 60 Actuations.

1 inhalation × 3 times daily = 3

Quantity supplied = 60

60 ÷ 3 = 20 days   Note: # (number of quantity dispensed)

MORE EXAMPLES ON DRUG DOSAGE CALCULATION

Example:1 Methadone 50mg by mouth is ordered. Methadone is available as 100mg per tab. How many tablets would be administered?

Tablets required = amount ordered ÷ amount available × quantity if any

Using the formula, 50mg ÷ 100mg

= 0.5mg

Example:2. If 50mg of a drug is required and your stock is 150mg in 6ml, what is the required dose?

Using the formula, 50 ÷ 150 × 6

= 2ml

Example: 3. Amoxicillin 125mg/5ml suspension, take 30mg by mouth on day one, then 50mg by mouth on days 2 through 5, dispensed quantity sufficient. How many ml should be dispensed to the patient?

125mg/5ml = 30mg/X

Cross multiply to solve for X

125X = 5 × 30

125X = 150

Divide both sides by 125 to find X

X = 1.2ml

125mg/5ml = 50mg/X

Cross multiply to solve for X

125X = 5 × 50

125X = 250

Divide both sides by 125 to find X

X = 2ml

4 days = 4 × 2

8ml

1.2ml + 8ml

= 9.2ml

Dosage calculation based on body weight:

A drug B 4mg/kg is ordered for a child who weighs 64.8 pounds. A drug B is available 500mg/4ml. How many milliliters of medication must be given?

Required dosage = weight(kg) × dosage ordered (per kg)

Convert 64.8 lb to kg

1kg = 2.2lb

Therefore 64.8 lb = 29.45kg

Using the formula, 29.45kg × 4mg/kg

= 117.8mg

500mg/4ml = 117.8mg/X

Cross multiply to solve for X

500X = 471.2

Divide both sides by 500

X = 0.9ml

Ratio and Proportion

1.If one capsule contains 400mg, how many mg are in 5 capsules?

$$\frac{400mg}{1\ cap} = \frac{X}{5\ caps}$$

By cross multiplying

X = 400 x 5

X = 2000mg.

2.Amanda D weighs 175 pounds. How much does she weigh in kilograms?

$$\frac{1kg}{X} = \frac{2.2\ Lb}{175\ Lb}$$

By cross multiplying

2.2 x X = 175 x 1

2.2X = 175

Divide both sides by 2.2 to find X

X = 79.55kg.

3.If 60 tablets cos t 120, how much would 30 tablets cost?

$$\frac{120}{60\ tabs} = \frac{X}{30\ tabs}$$

Cross multiply to solve for X

60X = 120 × 30

60X = 3600

Divide both sides by 60

X = 60

DOSAGE CALCULATIONS FORMULA:

Pediatric dosage

Using Clark's rule

A child's dose =

$$\frac{\text{Weight(lb)}}{150} \times \text{Adult dose}$$

Example 1. A child weighed 25 pounds, using a Clark's rule, calculate the dose of the child if the adult dose was 70 mg.

Change 25lb to kg

Using the formula, Child dose =

$$\frac{25}{150} \times 70\text{mg}$$

0.167 × 70mg

= 11.67mg.

Example 2. Calculate a child's dose if the weight of the child is 55kg and the adult dose is 60mg. Use the Clark's rule.

Firstly, change the kg to lb

2.2lb = lkg, so 55kg = 121 lb

Using the formula, child dose =

$$\frac{121}{150} \times 60\text{mg}$$

$0.4 \times 60\text{mg}$

$= 48.4\text{mg}$

Young's rule

Child's dose =

$$\frac{\text{Age}}{\text{Age} + 12} \times \text{Adult dose}$$

Note: Age in Years

Example: Calculate the child's dose if the adult dose is 45mg and the age of the child is 7 years. Use the Young's rule.

Using the formula, child's dose =

$$\frac{7}{7 + 12} \times 45\text{mg}$$

7/19 x 45mg

$0.37 \times 45\text{mg}$

$= 16.57\text{mg}.$

FRED'S RULE

Fred's rule =

$$\frac{\text{Age (mths)}}{150} \times \frac{\text{Adult dose}}{}$$

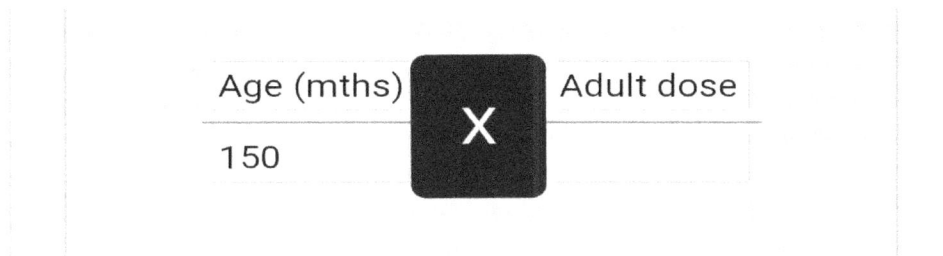

Example: A child who is 14 months old was admitted in a hospital. Calculate the child's dose if the adult dose is 90mg.

Using the formula, Child's dose =

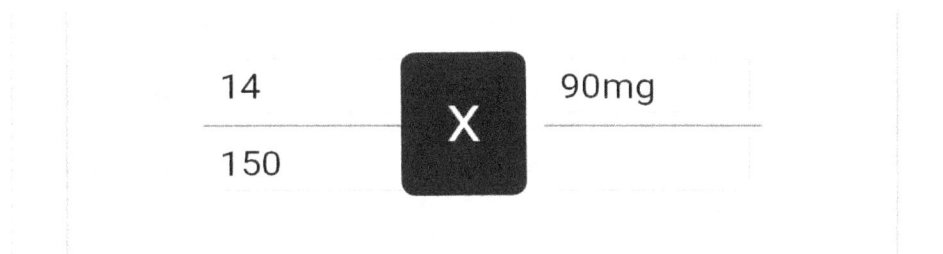

$$\frac{14}{150} \times \frac{90mg}{}$$

$0.09 \times 90mg$

= 8.4mg.

DILUTION/CONCENTRATIONS

Dilution/Concentration calculation = C1 × V1 = C2 × V2

Initial concentration C1

Final concentration C2

Initial Volume V1

Final Volume V2

Example: If 45% dextrose solution is diluted to 1450ml with water, find the new concentration of a 600ml.

Using the formula, C1 = 45%, V1 = 600ml, V2 = 1450ml, C2 = X

45 × 600 = 1450X

27000 = 1450X

Divide both sides by 1450

= 18.6%

Weight/Weight (w/w) concentration - solid dissolves in another solid calculated in grams; weight of solute divided by weight of solution.

Example: What is the w/w% of hydrocortisone if 20g of hydrocortisone is added to 250g of cold cream?

20g/250g

= 0.08 × 100

= 8%

Weight /Volume (w/v) concentration - solid dissolves in liquid whiles the weight is in grams and volume is in ml. Weight of solute divided by volume of solution.

Example: How many milligrams of Cefazolin powder are needed to prepare 1500ml of 0.06% w/v solution?

This number 0.06% = 0.06gm/100ml

Convert 0.06gm = 60mg.

$$\frac{60mg}{100ml} = \frac{X}{1500ml}$$

Cross multiply to solve for X

60 × 1500 = 100X

90000 = 100X

Divide both sides by 100

X = 900mg.

Volume/ Volume (v/v) concentration – liquid dissolves in another liquid calculated in ml. Volume of solute divided by volume of solution

Example: What is the amount of alcohol in 1 liter of an 80% solution?

$$\frac{80ml}{100ml} = \frac{Xml}{1000ml}$$

Cross multiply to solve for X

80 × 1000 = 100X

80000 = 100X

Divide both sides by 100

X = 800ml.

Specific gravity = weight of solute measured in gram ÷ volume of solution in ml. (1gm = 1ml)

What is the specific gravity of 400ml of liquid that weighs 200gm?

1ml = 1gm, 400ml = 400gm

Using the formula, 200gm ÷ 400gm

= 0.5

Intravenous calculations

How to find Rate:

Rate(ml/hr) = Volume(ml) ÷ Time(hr)

Example: A patient receives 1500ml of IV solution over 3 hours period. Calculate the flow rate.

Using the formula, rate = 1500 ÷ 3

= 500ml/hr

Example: Calculate the flow rate in ml/hr if a patient receives 0.45 liters of IV solution over a 3-hour period.

First, change liters to milliliters, 0.45 = 450ml

= 450 ÷ 3

150ml/hr.

How to find Volume:

Volume(ml) = Time(hr)× Rate(ml/hr)

Example: How many milliliters of IV solution would be needed to run an IV for 10 hours at a rate of 90ml/hr?

Using the formula, Volume = 90m/hr × 10hr

= 900ml

How to find Time:

Time(hr) = Volume(ml) ÷ Rate(ml/hr)

Example: How long will 2.4 liters last if an IV solution is run at 150ml/hr?

Firstly, change liters to milliliters, 2.4 liters = 2400ml

Using the formula, time = 2400ml ÷ 150ml/hr

= 16 hours.

How to find the drip or drop rate:

Drip Rate (drop per minutes) =

$$\frac{Volume(ml)}{Time\ (min)} \times Drop\ factor$$

Example: Find the gtts/min of the following iv solution to be run at

i.160ml/hr continuous using 10 gtts/ml tubing

ii.120ml/hr continuously using 15 gtt/ml tubing

Answer i. Drip Rate = 160ml/hr × 10 gtt/ml

Change 1 hour to minutes = 60

$$\frac{160\ ml}{60\ min} \times \frac{10\ gtt}{1\ ml}$$

160/6

= 26.67gtt/min

Answer ii. Drip Rate = 120ml/hr × 15 gtt/ml

$$\frac{120\ ml}{60\ min} \times \frac{15\ gtt}{1\ ml}$$

120/4

30gtt/min

More examples on IV calculations

1. An IV started at 2100 and programmed to run at 15gtt/min, containing a bag of 180mg of drug in a total of 1 liter of D5W. How much of the IV the patient would have received by 0200 if the infusion set is set to deliver 60gtt/ml?

15gtt/min ÷ 60gtt/ml = 4ml/min

9pm - 2am = 7hrs (2100 = 9pm, 0200 = 2am)

7 × 60 = 420 min

4ml × 420 = 1680ml

$$\frac{180mg}{1000ml} = \frac{Xmg}{1680ml}$$

Cross multiply to solve for X

$1000Xml = 180mg \times 1680ml$

$1000X = 302400mg$

Divide both sides by 1000

$X = 302.4mg$

2. An IV of 600ml of D5W to infuse at 45ml/hr. It is set to start at 0630. Find the infusion and completion time

$600ml/1 = 45ml/hr$

(hour to minute) = 60mins

$$\frac{600ml}{X} = \frac{45ml}{60min}$$

Cross multiply, $X = 36000 \div 45$

$X = 800$ minutes

$= 13.3$ hr

Change 0.3 to minutes. $0.3 \times 60 = 18$ minutes

$= 13hr\ 18min$

$06:30 + 13:18 = 19:18$

$24:00 - 19:18 = 04:82$

$= 04:82$

3. A volume of 2500ml of an IV solution is to infuse in 10hr using a 15gtt/ml set. Calculate the gtt/min flow rate

Drop/min = Volume(ml)/Time(min)× drop factor

= 2500ml/600min

= 2500ml/600min × 15gtt/ml

 = 62.5gtt/min

Alligation

Example 1. How many milliliters of solution prepared by mixing 50% and 20% IV solutions to make 300ml of a 30% alcohol solution?

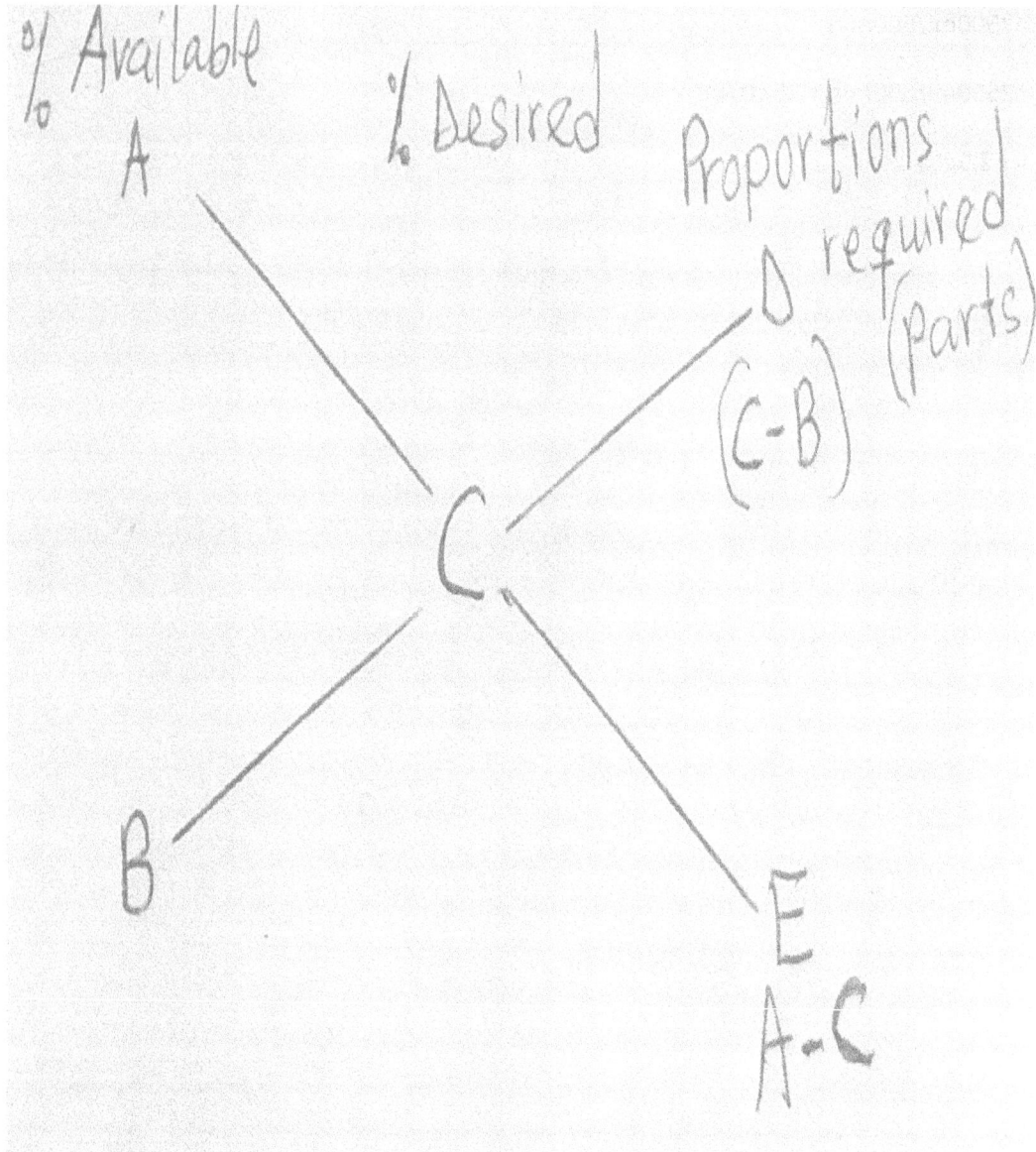

A = highest number, 50%

B = lowest number, 20%

C = middle number, 30%

D = 30 − 20 (C − B)

= 10

E = 50 – 30 (A – C)

= 20

Total Parts = 10 + 20 = 30

A (50% iv sol.) = 10 ÷ 30 × 300

= 100ml

E (20% iv sol.) = 20 ÷ 30 × 300

= 200ml

Example 2. How many milliliters of suspension should be mixed with 120mg/10ml and 60mg/10ml to prepare 300ml of a suspension of 10mg/ml?

Higher suspension 120mg/10ml = 12mg/ml

Lower suspension 60mg/10ml = 6mg/ml

Middle suspension 10mg/ml

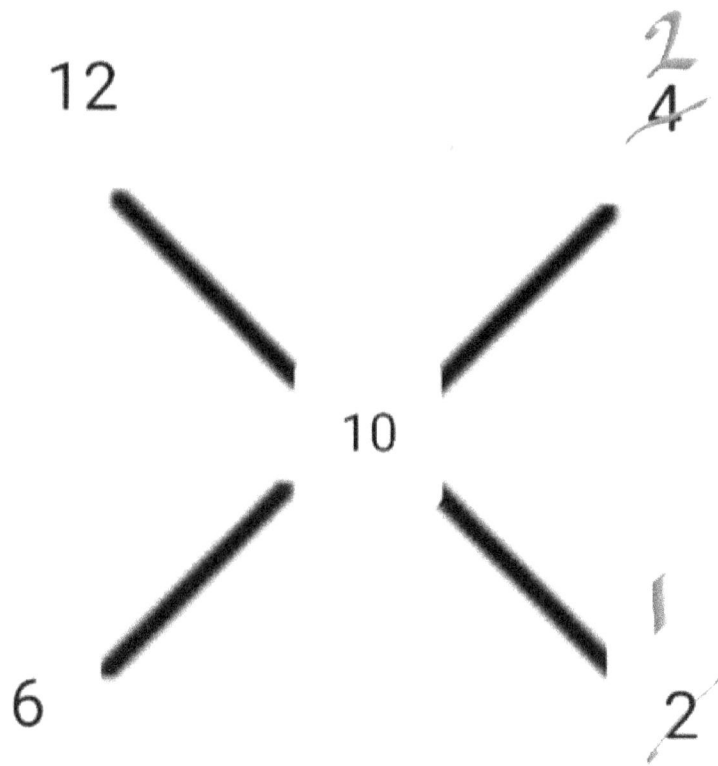

$$\begin{array}{ccc} 12 & & \overset{2}{4} \\ & 10 & \\ 6 & & \overset{1}{2} \end{array}$$

Higher part = 2

Lower part = 1

Total part of suspension 2 + 1 = 3

Higher suspension = 2/3 × 300

= 200ml

Lower suspension = 1/3 × 300

= 100ml

38

Capsule sizes chart

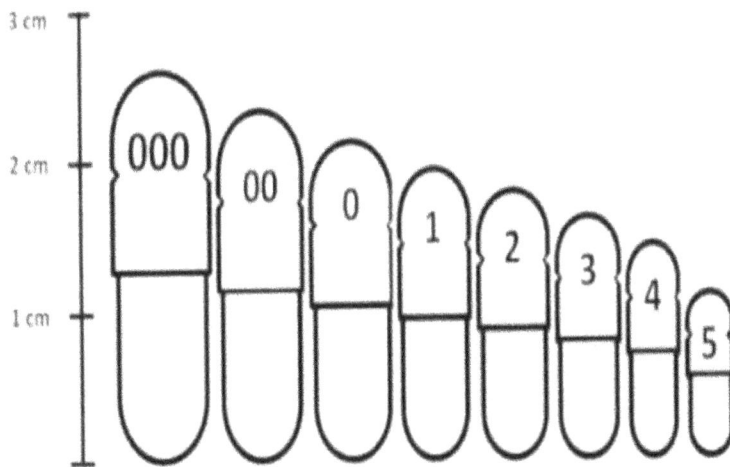

Take note: The smallest number is the largest capsule.

The diagram above illustrates the arrangement from the largest capsule to the smallest.

For example: 000 is the largest capsule and 5 is the smallest capsule.

Chapter 3

BUSINESS MATH

Gross Profit = Selling Price – Cost Price

Loss = Cost Price – Selling Price

Net profit = gross profit – dispensing fee.

Example: 1. A pharmacy sold a prescription drug for $ 59.00. The price of the drug was $ 37.00 from the wholesaler. What would be the gross profit?

Profit = Cost Price – Selling Price

= 59 – 37

= $ 22.00

Example: 2. If an Antipsychotic drug has AAC of $41.50, a retail price of $61.50 and a dispensing fee of $5.00. What's its net profit?

Hint: Retail price – Production cost – other expenses

61.50 – 41.50 – 5.00 = 15.00

Net Profit = $15.00

Markup percentage = Gross Profit ÷ Cost Price × 100

$$\frac{GProfit}{CPrice} \quad X \quad 100$$

Example: 3. A drug was sold by Albert Pharmacy for $ 450.00. The cost price was $ 340.00. Calculate the markup percentage.

Markup percentage = GP ÷ CP × 100

Hint: Find the gross profit first.

GP = CP - SP

= 450 – 340

= 110

The % markup

= 110 ÷ 340 x 100

= $ 32.35

Example: 4. A doctor prescribed a drug for a patient; Amoxicillin 250mg # 4. Your pharmacy has a 25% markdown and $6.00 dispensing fee. The wholesale price is $12.00 per capsule. Find the retail price for this prescription of 4 capsules.

12 × 4 = $48.00

48 × 25/100

48 × 0.25

= $12.00

48 – 12 = $36.00

36 + 6[dispensing fee] = $42.00

Take note: Markup – add and Markdown – subtract

Example 5. A drug A that regularly sells for $9.00 is marked down to $5.75. What is the discount rate?

Original Price – Markdown Price ÷ Original Price X 100

$9.00 – $5.75 = 3.25

3.25 ÷ 9.00 = 0.36

Find the percentage of 0.36

0.36 × 100 = 36%

The markdown is 36%

Example 6. A drug M originally prices at $45.00 is marked off 25%. What is the sale price?

Mark off price

= 45 x 25/100

= 45 x 0.25

= 11.25

Sale Price = 45 − 11.25 = $33.75

Example 7. What is the markup for a drug C that costs $10.00, has a dispensing fee of $1.75 and retails for $17.85?

Retail price − Cost Price

$17.85 − $10.00

= $7.85

*In this problem, markup is also gross profit.

Take note: Discount amount = Selling Price − Discount%

Discounted Price = Selling Price − Discount amount.

Chapter 4

PHARMACY LAW AND REGULATIONS

Some organizations in the health sectors:

FDA - Food and Drug Administration(1906): regulates ,approves and processes registration and recalls

OBRA 90 – Omnibus Budget Reconciliation Act: provides health care plans.

HIPAA – Health Insurance Portability and Accountability Act (1996): security and privacy.

OSHA – Occupational Safety and Health Act (1970): MSDS for chemical and hazardous materials.

DEA – Drug Enforcement Agency: investigates control substances/issues DEA numbers

BOP – Board of Pharmacy: regulates pharmacists/technicians and sets state laws and requirements.

FDCA – Food and Drug Cosmetic Act: replaces FDA of 1906, clarifies misbranding, adulterations.

DHA – Durham Humphrey Amendment (1951): differentiates between OTC and Legend drugs (prescription drugs). It ensures CAUTION: " Federal law prohibits dispensing without a prescription" label written on each prescription drug.

CMEA – Combat Methamphetamine Epidemic Act: regulates OTC drugs for pseudoephedrine. Daily 3.6gms, Monthly 9gms, Mailing 7.5gms

PPPA – Poison Prevention Packaging Act of 1970: requires locking caps.

KHA – Kefauver-Harris Amendment of 1962: ensures effectiveness and safety of drugs

CSA - Control Substance Act: replaces Harrison's act.

USP 795- United States Pharmacopeia 795: non sterile compounding.

USP 797- United States Pharmacopeia 797: sterile compounding.

TJC- The Joint Commission: improves quality and safety in the health sectors.

ASHP – American Society of Health-System Pharmacists.

Orphan Drug Act (1983) – established specifically for the treatment of rare diseases.

Reference books:

RED BOOK - contains prices of medications

ORANGE BOOK – contains therapeutic equivalent/prescription drugs.

THE PHYSICIAN DESK REFERENCE (PDR) - contains package insert of prescription drugs

IDENT-A-DRUG – contains brand, generic name and manufacturer.

THE PHARMACY TECHNICIAN'S POCKET DRUG REFERENCE – contains illustrations, brand and generic names, therapeutic classes and uses, strength and dosage form.

TRISSEL'S HANDBOOK ON INJECTABLE DRUGS – contains information on injectable drugs in USA and internationally.

PEDIATRIC AND NEONATAL DOSAGE HANDBOOK – contains information and evaluation on pediatric patients.

CONTROLLED SUBSTANCES

Controlled Substances Act implemented a drug classification based on its abuse and safety ranging from C1 to C5. These are known as schedule drugs.

<u>**Drug Classifications**</u>.

Drug Schedule 1 [C1] – most potential for abuse, no medicinal value. They are the most dangerous among the Schedule drugs.

Marijuana*

Ecstasy

Heroin

Peyote

Methaqualone

* this drug has medicinal value and it's been approved in some states but it has not been approved by federal.

Drug Schedule 2 [C2]– high potential abuse, some medicinal value. These drugs are also considered to be dangerous.

Cocaine

Vicodin

Adderall

Oxycontin

Meperidine

Methadone

Drug Schedule 3 [C3]– moderate potential for abuse.

Testosterone

Anabolic steroids

Drug Schedule 4 [C4]– low potential for abuse

Valium

Xanax

Tramadol

Soma

Ambien

Drug Schedule 5 [C5] – least potential for abuse.

Robitussin

Ezogabine

Motofen

 Lyrica

DEA VERIFICATION

B   Hospital/Clinic

C   Practitioner

M   Mid-level practitioner

E   Manufacturer

F   Distributor

DEA NUMBERS

Example 1: BK3410254.

K is the last name of the Practitioner

3 + 1 + 2 = 6

4 + 0 + 5 = 9, multiply **2 by 9** equal to **18, 6 + 18 = 24.** Therefore **4** is the last DEA NUMBER

Example 2: MR 2173401

R is the last name of the Mid – Level Practitioner

2 + 7 + 4 = 13

1 + 3 + 0 = 4 , 4 × 2 = 8, 13 + 8 = 21, therefore **1** is the last DEA NUMBER

DEA FORMS

DEA 222: Order form, valid for 60 days. This form has 3 copies:

Brown copy – for supplier

Green copy – for DEA

Blue copy – for Pharmacy

DEA 224: Registration form.

DEA 41: Destruction form, submitted each year.

DEA 106: Loss/Theft form.

DEA 225: Form needed to manufacture or distribute controlled substances.

PHARMACY DEA'S PERMIT lasts for 3 years while DEA receipts for destruction must be maintained for 2 years.

SCH. C2 - Medications can be kept on file for 2 years, no refill and no expiration.

SCH. C3- C4 - Medications can be refilled 5 times for 6 months after the date of issue.

SCH. C5 - Unlimited refill

Controlled substances Prescription File Systems

1. Two-file system: one file contains all C2 prescriptions and other file contains all other prescriptions. In this file system a red C stamps are placed on C3, C4 and C5 prescriptions to differentiate between them and the non-controlled medications.

2. Other two-file system: all controlled substances are placed in one folder and other non-controlled prescriptions are placed in different folder. C3, C4 and C5 prescriptions must still have a red C stamp placed on them.

3. Three-file system: the pharmacy has 3 files, one file contains C2, second one for C3 – C4 and third one for non-controlled prescriptions.

LEGEND DRUGS: Prescription drugs.

NON-LEGEND DRUGS: Over-the-counter drugs (OTC)

RESTRICTED DRUGS

Thalidomide – to treat and prevent skin diseases. This drug can cause death and deformity

Isotretinoin – treats severe acne

Clozapine - treats schizophrenia

Clinical trials

A clinical trial is a research study performed to evaluate a new drug or device. This research is classified into phases of studies

Phase 1. This is the initial phase of testing which involves small group of healthy people. It's designed to determine the effect of a drug on humans. It is based on collection of data.

Phase 2. This phase of study tests the efficacy of a drug. It involves hundreds of patients being divided into 2. One group receives the experimental drug while other receives standard treatment or placebo. In this phase, side effects are analyzed.

Phase 3. This is a large-scale testing which involves thousands of patients. This stage is carried out to analyze the effectiveness and the benefits of the drug. After this phase, a pharmaceutical company can request FDA approval for marketing its drug.

Phase 4. This is the post marketing surveillance trial stage whereby a drug has been approved for sale. The following are performed at this stage:

comparison of drugs

monitoring the effectiveness of a drug over long period of time.

determining the cost-effectiveness of a drug.

Investigational New Drugs:

A patient can take investigational drugs when all medications have failed. The prescriber of this investigational drugs must follow certain protocols and must be approved by FDA.

Therapeutic Equivalent – when medications have the same clinical effect and safety profile.

Medications are therapeutically equivalent if they have:

Same strength/concentration

Same dosage form

Same route of administration

Same active ingredients

And they must also be:

Correctly labeled

Bioequivalent

Same and effective

Manufactured in accordance with FDA regulations

These drugs do not necessarily need to have:

Color

Shape

Packaging

Flavor

Preservatives

Chapter 5

STERILE AND NON STERILE COMPOUNDING

STERILE COMPOUNDING

Is a mixture of 2 or more ingredients for parenteral route of administration use.

This is type of compounding is very strict and must follow strict guidelines otherwise a least mistake can cause harm/infection or even death. PPE must be worn according to specific guidelines. Some of the PPEs are as follow:

Lab coats/suits

Shoe covers

Gloves

Mask

Bouffant caps

Goggles.

A compounding pharmacy technician begins by:

putting on shoe covers

wearing hair cover or bouffant cap

wearing mask

washing hands

wearing gown (before entering the clean room)

washing hands again by using 70% isopropyl alcohol

putting on gloves.

EQUIPMENT USED FOR STERILE COMPOUNDING

Isopropyl alcohol 70%

Ampules

Filter needle

Infusion pump

Vial

Roll clamp

Needle adapter

Compounding log

Ampule breaker

Flexible bag

Filter straw

Heparin lock

Drip chamber

HEPA FILTERS AND LAMINAR FLOW HOODS are certified every 6 months

CLASS 1 HEPA FILTERING SYSTEM - Filters air until the air becomes exhausted.

CLASS 2 HEPA FILTERING SYSTEM - Filters the exhaust air.

CLASS 3 HEPA FILTERING SYSTEM - Contains chemical/hazardous substances.

Garbing takes place in the anteroom.

Anteroom is the area where preparation takes place.

NON STERILE COMPOUNDING

Non sterile compounding is also called extemporaneous compounding -

Is a mixture of 2 or more ingredients for enteral route of administration use.

REASON FOR COMPOUNDING

to reduce or increase the strength of the drug.

add flavor.

change the route of administration.

ASEPTIC TECHNIQUE

good hygiene

handwashing

Personal Protective Equipment (PPE)

Type of Dispersions

Ointment   -   Oily form

Cream -   Thick/semi solid

Solution - Liquid preparation

Suspension - Liquid and solid particles

Tablet   - Compressed/molded solid

Capsule - Gelatin form

Suppository - Conical/cylindrical shape.

Anhydrous - Insoluble in water but absorb water from the atmosphere

Oleaginous - Insoluble in water but do not absorb water from the atmosphere

Geometric dilution. – the process of mixing 2 ingredients with unequal quantities.

Trituration – the process of grinding powder to form fine particles.

Tincture - alcoholic extract made from herbs or animals.

Elixir - sweetener, water and alcohol mixed together to form solution.(Syrups)

Reconstitution – the process of mixing powder and water together to form suspension.

Reconstituted statins drugs in the form of antibiotics/capsules/tablets last for 10 days. However other products not made with water last for 6 months unless one ingredient has an earlier beyond use date.

Oral solution with water good for 14 days.

Topical solution, ointments and creams good for 30 days.

Sign of incompatibility

Precipitation

Color change

Cloudiness

Separation.

Measuring and Weighing devices

Class A balance

Counter balance

Cylindrical graduated cylinder

Conical graduated cylinder

Class A balance features:

Sensitivity = 6mg

Capacity = 120mg

Counter balance features:

Sensitivity = 100mg

Capacity = 5kg

Class A balances are certified every year (12 months).

Parts of syringe and needle

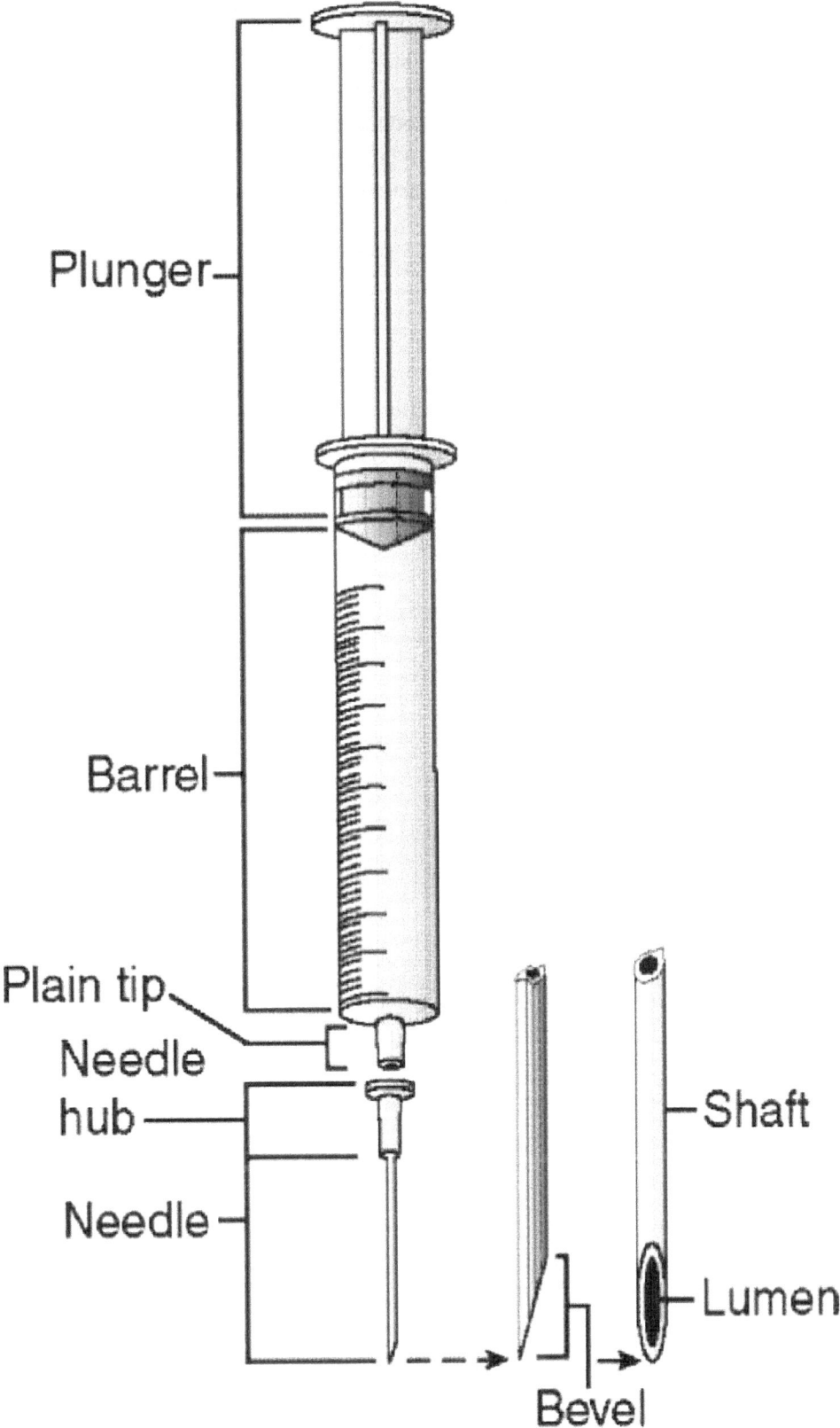

Plunger

Barrel

Plain tip

Needle hub

Needle

Shaft

Lumen

Bevel

Needle Recapping

A needle should never be left on the desk after use or held close to the body. It should be disposed of in to a sharp container. Recapping a needle is very risky, on a safer side, it's advisable to dispose needle immediately after use. However, if you are required to recap a needle this method below should be used to avoid injuries. The needle recapping is done by using mechanical devices such as tongs, forceps or one-handed scoop method. The following steps should be taken when using one-handed scoop method:

Place the needle on the desk

Using one hand, slightly insert the needle into the cap.

Other needle Recapping devices allow easy recapping.

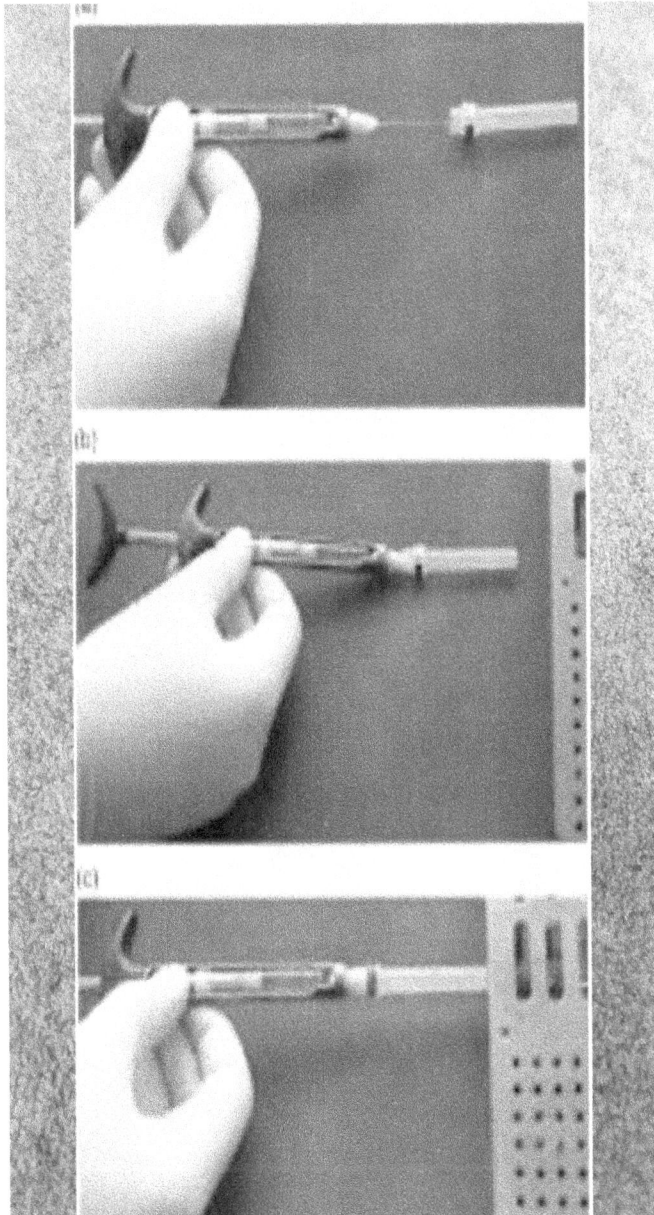

Delrin Acetal
Resin Needle
Recapper

Multi Needle
Recapper

Needle Safe II
Recapper

Stainless Steel
Needle Recapper

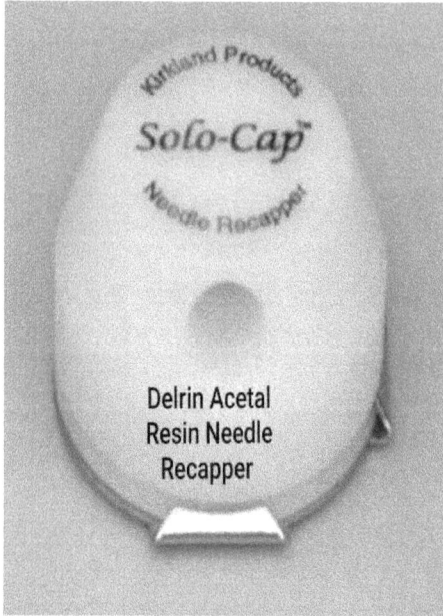

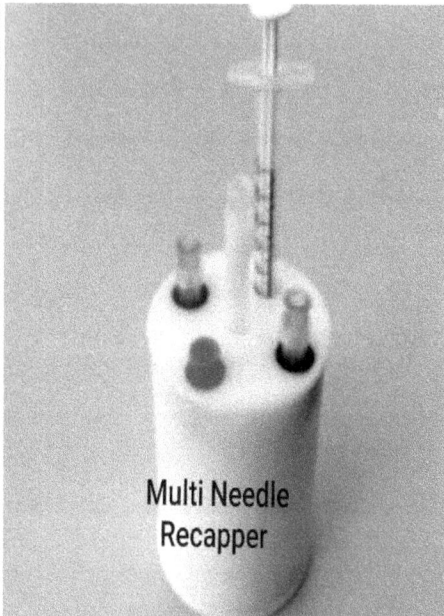

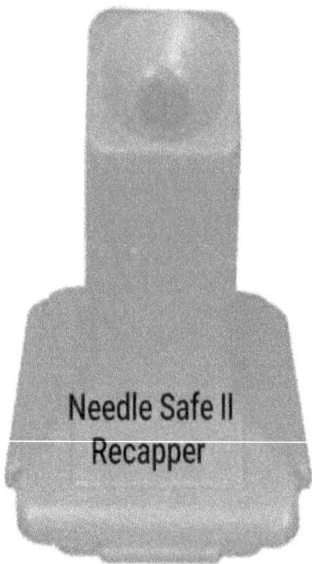

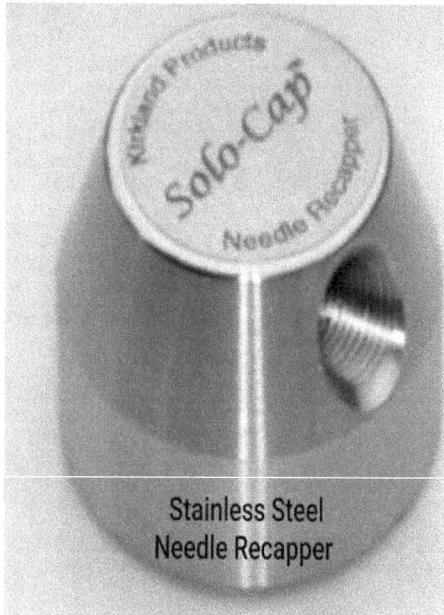

SOME OF THE NEEDLE RECAPPERS

Chapter 6

MEDICATION SAFETY

Medication errors are errors that occur during and after prescribing and administering of drugs.

Forms of medication error

Prescribing error   -   incorrect medications ordered by a prescriber

Wrong time error -   schedule time frame not fulfilled

Unauthorized drug error - unauthorized prescriber/wrong drug being administered.

Omission error -   medications do not follow sequentially.

Deteriorated drug error -   expired drugs being used.

INSTITUTE OF SAFE MEDICATION PRACTICES

ISMP educates health workers about medication errors and prevention. Some of the programs are as follows:

MERP - Medication Error Reporting Program

MEDMARX - internet accessible data base to track medication errors[overseen by USP]

Risk management and guidelines

How to prevent medication errors.

Using barcode verification

Using labeled storage bins or bin dividers

Using tall man letters

Using CPOE (Computerized Physician Order Entry)

Providing sufficient space for drugs to permit segregation

Question ambiguous orders

Ask questions if you are not familiar with the abbreviations.

Make sure prescription and orders are correctly spelled.

Medications and orders should be reviewed 3 times.

Errors to avoid in Decimal point placement

Make sure decimal points are more visible.

Never use a whole number with a decimal point and a trailing zero. For instance, Amoxicillin 5.0mg could be misinterpreted as 50mg which can lead to overdose and even death.

Decimal point should never be left alone but always start with a zero. For instance, Heparin .9mg could easily misinterpreted as 9mg.

Note: Check and verify all faxed prescriptions, decimal points may not be visible.

Tall man lettering (look alike/sound alike)

Tall man letters are used to distinguish difference in spelling between 2 or more similarly spelled drug names. FDA approves tall man letters.

Look alike/ sound alike medications

Acetazolamide	Acetohexamide
Bupropion	Bus**PIR**one
ALPRAZolam	**LOR**azepam
ARIPiprazole	**RABE**prazole
car**BAM**azepine	**Ox**carbazepine
Cele**XA**	Cele**BREX**
Clonaze**PAM**	Clo**NID**ine
Clomi**PHENE**	Clomi**PRAMINE**
DULoxetine	**FLU**oxetine
Met**FORMIN**	Metro**NIDAZOLE**

High alert medications classes

Chemotherapy agent

Antiarrhythmic

Insulin

Antithrombotic agent

Anticoagulant

Hypoglycemic oral

Anesthetic agent

Medication error reporting codes:

A - No error

B - Error occurred but did not reach patients

C - Error reached patients but no harm

D - Error reached patients, no harm but needed attention

E - Error, temporary harm

F - Error, temporary harm/prolonged hospitalization

G - Error, permanent harm

H - Error, harm, required hospitalization to save life

I - Error, death

Pregnancy Category codes:

A - No risk, safe.

B - No risk

C - Benefits might be greater than the risk involved.

D - Benefit is greater than the risks

X - Risk is greater than the benefits.

The five rights of a patient

right drug

right time

right dose

right patient

right route

Chapter 7

PHARMARCY QUALITY ASSURANCE

Organizations that promote quality assurance are:

FDA

USP

TJC

ISMP

ASHP

APHA

BOP

FDA – approves and clears all medical devices. Provides post-market surveillance on medical devices.

Evaluates radiating emitting products.

Establishes clinical trials.

Provides information on drug shortages and safety.

Evaluates the safety of drug products.

Oversees all allergenic products.

Oversees MEDWATCH.

Ensures required labeling of drugs

FDA DRUG RECALLS

Drug Recall class 1 – serious adverse effects that lead to injury or death.

Drug Recall class 2 – temporarily adverse effects.

Drug Recall class 3 – no adverse effect but violets FDA regulations.

USP - Establishes standard for sterile and non sterile compounding

Ensures quality, strength, identity and purity of medicines, food ingredients and dietary supplements.

Establishes requirements for labeling of medications.

TJC - Establishes national patient safety goals.

Accredits health care sectors

Ensures safe environment for patients and workers

Provides certification for disease specific care.

Improves quality and safety

Makes "DO NOT USE" list.

ASHP - Improves medications use for patient safety.

Provides professional advocacy on health system on pharmacy issues.

Supports professional practices of pharmacists in hospitals and health system set ups.

Risk for pharmacy sterile products: (ASHP)

Level 1. Products should be completely administered within 28 hours.

Level 2. Products should be stored and administered not more than 28 hours.

Level 3 .Open system transfer should be used for products from multiple ingredients.

ISMP – Provides resources such as:

Black Box warning

Tall man letters

High alert medications

Medication safety

Error prone abbreviations

Oversees MERP

 Do not crush list.

Some of "Do not crush" list medications

Bayer…………….Aspirin (enteric-coated)

Aciphex…………Rabeprazole (slow-release)

Ambien…………Zolpidem (slow-release)

Cardizem……….Diltiazem (slow-release)

Cardura…………Doxazosin (slow-release)

Depakote………Divalproex (slow-release)

Dexilant………..Dexlansoprazole (slow-release)

Ms contin……..Morphine (slow-release)

Oxycontin……..Oxycodone (slow-release)

Paxil……………Paroxetine (slow-release)

Prevacid……..Lansoprazole (slow-release)

Prilosec………Omeprazole (slow-release)

Requip………..Ropinirole (slow-release)

Ultram…………Tramadol (slow-release)

Xanax…………..Alprazolam (slow-release)

Reasons why some of the medications should not be crushed

Because of its:

taste

liquid contents

dosage forms (slow and extended release and enteric-coated)

irritation of the mucous membrane

BOP - 1. Sets standard for licensing of pharmacy technicians and pharmacists

2. Ensures specific requirements are met.

OSHA - Responsible for safety through education and assistance by providing material safety data sheet(MSDS) for chemical hazardous materials.

OBRA 87 – Responsible for Medicare and Medicaid in long-term facilities and pharmacies.

OBRA 90 - Requires that all pharmacists must perform drug utilization evaluation.

Drug Utilization Review is a review of a drug that's prescribing, dispensing and the use of medication to determine its effectiveness or any health related issues.

APhA- 1 Provides informational resources for pharmacy technicians and the pharmacists

2.Improves medications and patient care.

MAR. - Medications Administration Report – legal records of drugs administered.

TAR. - Treatment Administration Report – records of various treatments.

Center for disease control, CDC is responsible for reducing the spread of infectious diseases.

CDC must be notified if employee is exposed to pathogens at work

Hypoallergenic gloves should be changed every hour.

Drug reconciliation – checking on patients during the time of medications to see how they are faring or doing.

Communication channels

Communication plays a vital role in the health sectors. Effectiveness of communication can reduce errors being made. Here is the list of channels of communication from the most effective to the least.

Face-to-face

Telephone

E-mail

Written memo

Letters

Posted notice

Bulletins

Chapter 8

MEDICATION ORDER ENTRY AND FILL PROCESS

THE DO'S OF PHARMACY TECHNICIAN

Ensures health and safety of the patients.

Assists and supports pharmacist.

Maintains competency.

Prepares medicine for patients.

Provides information to patients

Assists with insurance claims processing

Stocks and prices medications

Receives and verifies prescription.

DONT'S

Perform counseling

Perform the final check-up of prescription

Taking new prescriptions

Consultation with providers

PRESCRIPTIONS ON CONTROLLED SUBSTANCES.

Prescriptions for controlled substances on schedule 2 must be handwritten in ink or indelible pencil or typewritten and it cannot be faxed/telephoned unless in an emergency situation whereby the prescriber has to submit written information within 7 days. The prescriber must sign manually.

Prescription for schedule 3, 4 and 5 controlled substances can be written, oral or by fax.

A prescription drug can be faxed, sent electronically, present in person and must be handwritten on hard copy and signed by the prescriber. All prescriptions are required to have the statement, Caution: "Federal Law prohibits dispensing without a prescription" written on the hard copy.

Hard copy of prescription has these specific information:

Name of the patient

Date of birth

Phone number

Prescriber's name/address/phone number

Signature

Information required from a prescriber

Name

NPI number

Office address

State license

DEA number

The information required on prescription of controlled substances:

DEA number on the original copy

Prescriber's address

The patient's address

Number of refills if allowed

Quantity

Directions for use

Manual signature of the physician

Date the prescription was written.

Drug name

Dosage form

Date of issue

Patient profile information requirement

Name of the patient

Any medication currently taken

Any allergy

Medical history

Therapeutic duplication

History of drug abuse

Insurance information.

Prescription label information requirement

Date of the prescription written

Name and address of the pharmacy

Patient's name

Prescriber's name

Generic/brand of the prescription

Drug manufacturer's name

Dosage strength

Number of drugs

Expiration date

Initial of the pharmacist

Refill information

Repackaged medication information requirement

Name of medications

Name of the drug manufacturer

Strength and dosage form

Lot number

Beyond-use-date

Medication order label information

The filled date

The name and address of the pharmacist

Name of the patient

Generic and brand of medication

The strength of the medication

Number of drugs

Prescriber's name

The name of the manufacturer

Pharmacist initials

Number of refills allowed

Patient package insert information

Name of the drug

Description of medication

Date of drug approval

Indications and usage

Contraindications

Warning and precautions

Storage information

Overdose, dosage and administration

Medication that requires package insert

Isotretinoin

Estrogen

Progesterone

Oral contraceptives

A lot number is assigned to a particular batch of drugs by the manufacturer.

Types of containers:

Hermetic container - protects the content from air/gas

Light resistant container – protects the content from light

Single dose container – for parenteral administration use

Tight container – protects the content from contamination.

Well closed container – protects the content from being lost.

Single unit container – holds quantity for single dose.

Oral contraceptives are excluded from child-resistant containers policy

DAW CODES

DAW 0 – No brand is selected, substitute accepted.

DAW1 – Brand medication necessarily by doctor.

DAW 2- Patient requested.

DAW 3 - Pharmacist selected.

DAW 4- Out of stock, substitute

DAW 5- Brand dispensed, priced as generic

DAW 6 – Override

DAW 7-   brand name mandated by law.

DAW 8- Generic not available, substitute.

DAW 9 – Other.

NATIONAL DRUG CODES

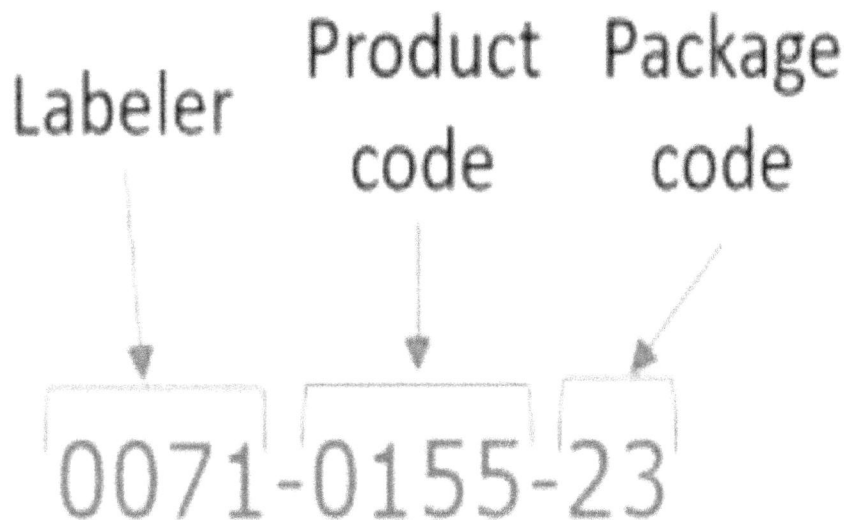

NDC numbers are used to order and verify drugs during dispensing and inventory.

Take note: Many NDCs are displayed in 10-digit format on drug packaging however the proper billing requires 11-digit format (5-4-2).

How to convert 10-digit to 11-digit of NDC

You can convert a 10-digit to a 11-digit of NDC by placing **zero** in the beginning of any of the segment which is **5-4-2** format.

Example 1: 0071-0155-23 …………………This is a 10-digit which has 4-4-2 format.

Using 5-4-2 format, we need to place the zero at the beginning of the first segment since the second segment has 4 digits and the third segment has 2 digits.

00071-0155-23 is the 11-digit.

Example 2: 34210-586-37…………………5-3-2 format.

Using 5-4-2 format, we place the zero at the beginning of the second segment.

34210-0586-37 is the 11-digit.

NDC 12345-365-97

The first set is the manufacturer/labeler – the company

The second set is the product

The last set is the package – the dose.

Inscription - name of the medications and the strength.

Subscription - information to inform the pharmacists about a particular medication.

Sig - direction of the medications to be taken.

Temperature conversion formula: **5f = 9c + 160**

Freezer : -20 to -10 degree Celsius

Refrigerator (Cold): 2 to 8 degree Celsius

Cool : 8 to 15 degree Celsius

Room temperature : temperature at working area.

Control room temperature : 20 to 25 degree Celsius.

Warm : 30 to 40 degree Celsius

Chapter 9

PHARMACY INVENTORY MANAGEMENT

Inventory process and tools:

Just-in-time ordering - drugs are ordered as demanded.

Periodic Automatic Replacement (PAR)- automatic ordering system.

Types of inventory

Initial inventory – inventory on a new pharmacy or change of pharmacist.

Biennial - inventory done every 2 years.

Perpetual - inventory done on what is on hand or available at that particular time.

FORMULARY

Closed formulary - drugs not listed require prior authorization or may not be covered.

Open formulary - drugs listed to be covered.(approved drugs)

Stock rotation is the arrangement of products in such a way that old products are sold before the new products.

Inventory turnover is how inventory is being sold or used over a given period of time.

Inventory turnover rate = total sale ÷ average inventory

Example: Albert Pharmacy has an initial inventory of $20,000.00 and final inventory of $60,000.00. Calculate the turnover rate if the total sale is one million.

First of all, find the average inventory

= initial + final inventory divided by 2

= $20,000.00 + 60,000.00

= $80,000.00 ÷ 2

= $40,000.00

Now find the turnover rate

Using the formula, total sale/average inventory

= $1,000,000.00 ÷ $40,000.00

= 25

Chapter 10

PHARMACY BILLING AND REIMBURSEMENT

Reimbursement formula = cost + dispensing fee

Managed care reimbursement = Average Wholesale Price (AWP) - % discount + dispensing fee

Actual cost pharmacy paid = Actual Acquisition Cost (AAC) + dispensing fee.

Generic reimbursement = Maximum Allowable Cost(MAC) + dispensing fee .

BANK IDENTIFICATION NUMBER (BIN) - A six digit number used to identify a company for reimbursement of the pharmacy for the prescription being filled.

Medicare and Medicaid

Centers for Medicare and Medicaid Services (CMS) oversees Medicare and Medicaid.

Medicare is the largest medical benefits established in 1965.

Parts of Medicare

Medicare part A - covers inpatient hospital stays, care in hospice and nursing homes(hospital insurance)

Medicare part B – covers doctor's appointment, out patients, medical supplies and preventive services.

Medicare part C - covers Medicare Advantage Plans which comprises Medicare part A(Inpatient services) and part B(Outpatient services). Some of the plans are Health Maintenance Organizations (HMO), Preferred Provider Organizations (PPO), Fee for Services.

HMO – is a type of health care that requires you to select a primary care doctor and a referral to see a specialist.

PPO – is a type of health care whereby you can go to any doctor or hospital of your choice but it's cheaper if you select from the same network.

Tricare is the insurance plan for the military personnel and their families

Medicare part D - covers prescription drugs.

Tips to memorize the Medicare parts, practice this below it's helpful:

Look for the **HOSPITAL** first and make an **APPOINTMENT.** You will be asked for your **MEDICAL ADVANTAGE PLAN/ INSURANCE** to process your **PRESCRIPTION DRUGS.**

A for Hospital

B for Appointment

C for Medical Plan/Insurance

D for Prescription drugs

Medicaid - for those who have low income, blind, disabled and pregnant women. It's funded by federal and state governments.

Online Adjudication – processing of a prescription claim to a third-party provider.

Coordination of benefits – the process whereby 2 insurance companies come together to pay claims for a client.

Insurance claim codes:

01 - card owner

02 - for spouse

03 - children/dependent

00 - no code is selected

Bill payment responsibilities

Patient pays co pay and deductible.

Pharmacy takes prescription drugs cost and dispensing fees from the insurance.

Insurance pays the remaining amount of the bill.

First Tier Drugs -   Generic name drugs that have the lowest co-pay.

Second Tier Drugs - Brand name drugs that have the moderate co-pay.

Third Tier Drugs -   Non formulary drugs which have the highest co-pay.

Prescription rejection codes	Description
1	Invalid/missing BIN
2	Invalid/missing version number
3	Invalid/missing transaction code
4	Invalid/missing PCN
5	Invalid/missing pharmacy number
6	Invalid/missing group number
7	Invalid/missing cardholder ID number
8	Invalid/missing person code
9	Invalid/missing date of birth
10	Invalid/missing patient gender code
11	Invalid/missing patient relationship code
12	Invalid/missing patient location
13	Invalid/missing other coverage code
14	Invalid/missing eligibility clarification code
15	Invalid/missing date of service
16	Invalid/missing prescription or service reference number
17	Invalid/missing fill number
19	Invalid/missing day supply
20	Invalid/missing compound code
21	Invalid/missing service identification number
22	Invalid/missing DAW code
23	Invalid/missing ingredient cost submitted
25	Invalid/missing prescriber ID
26	Invalid/missing unit of measure
28	Invalid/missing date prescription written
29	Invalid/missing number of refill authorized
32	Invalid/missing level of service
33	Invalid/missing prescription origin code

34	Invalid/missing submission clarification code
35	Invalid/missing primary care provider ID number
38	Invalid/missing basis of cost
39	Invalid/missing diagnosis code
40	Pharmacy not contracted with plan on date of service
41	Submit bill to other processor or primary payer
50	Non-matched pharmacy number
51	Non-matched group ID
52	Non-matched cardholder ID
53	Non-matched person code
54	Non-matched product or service ID number
55	Non-matched product package size
56	Non-matched prescriber ID
58	Non-matched primary prescriber
60	Product or service not covered for patient age
61	Product or service not covered for patient gender
62	Mismatched patient or cardholder ID name
63	Institutionalized patient product or service not covered
64	Claim submitted does not match prior authorization
65	Patient is not covered
66	Patient age exceeds maximum age
67	Filled before coverage effective
68	Filled after coverage expired
69	Filled after coverage terminated
70	Product or service not covered

Third party prescription insurance card information

Group number

BIN number

Subscriber number

PCN (Processor Control Number)

Person code

Help desk number

Chapter 11

PHARMACY INFORMATION SYSTEM USAGE AND APPLICATIONS

List of computer input devices

Mouse

Keyboard

Scanner

Microphone

Digital pen

Digital camera

List of computer output devices

Monitor

Plotters

Printer

Speaker

Headphone

Projector

Other important parts of computer are as follows:

Memory – temporarily workspace

Processor – brains of the computer

Storage – where information is stored permanently

Modem – convert signal for communication.

Interface – connection between 2 or more computers

Database of information on a computer system backed up daily.

AUTOMATION SYSTEMS IN THE COMMUNITY AND HOSPITAL PHARMACY SETTING.

ScriptPro (community pharmacy) – an automated counting device that receives prescription, picks exact drugs, count, does the packaging and labeling.

Baker cell (community pharmacy) - an automated counting device that uses bar codes to read prescription label to dispense.

Kirby Lester (community pharmacy) – an automated counting device that uses scanning and touch screen system for counting and verifying medications.

Robot-Rx (hospital pharmacy) – an automated counting device that uses bar codes reader to read and package medications for delivery.

Moreover, Pyxis, medRover, medTower, medSelect flex and medCarousel are also automated systems.

Chapter 12

PHARMACY TERMINOLOGY

Antacid ………….. relieves from acid

Analgesics……….. Pain killers

Antidepressants……..against depression

Anticoagulants……… against blood clotting

Antidiabetic…..   fight to lower blood sugar

Antipyretics ……….fight fever

Interferons………..attack viruses

Vasodilators……….chest pain/hypertension

Glucocorticoids………inflammation

Decongestants………mucous/phlegm removal

SSRI…………for depression

Antiemetics……….stop vomiting

Anticonvulsants…….against seizures

Antitussive………against cough

Benzodiazepines…….. anxiety

Bronchodilators………relax bronchial smooth muscles.

Anticholinergic………reduce muscle spasm in intestines.

Bactericidal………kill bacteria

Bacteriostatic……….slow down growth of bacteria.

Intradermal……….top layer of the skin.

Otic…… for the ear

Ophthalmic……for the eye

Sublingual………under the tongue.

Intramuscular........through the muscle

Intravenous..........through the veins

Brady ....slow

Hypoglycemia..........low blood glucose level

Hyperkalemia......... concentration of potassium in the blood

Tachy..........fast

Contraceptive.............prevent pregnancy

Subcutaneous............under the skin

Buccal ....inside the cheek

Intranasal....................through the nose

Rectal........................into the rectum

Brand name ....proprietary name

Generic name...............scientific name

Suffix List

-pril....................ACE Inhibitor

-asone/olone......Steroid

-zepam/zolam.......Benzodiazepine

-caine....................local anesthetic

-mycin/cillin/cycline/floxacin......Anti-biotic

-prazole..............Proton Pump Inhibitor

-vir........................Anti-viral

-nazole...............Anti-fungal

-dipine...............Calcium ch. Block

-olol...................Beta blocker

-sartan................A2RB

-statin……………….Cholesterol

Ceph-/cef- [prefix]……Anti-biotic

-fenac…………………..NSAID

-onide…………………..Corticosteroids

-zosin…………………..Alpha blockers

Chapter 13

PTCE PRACTICE QUESTIONS

1. Which of the following can be a substitute for Zestril?

A Prilosec

B Vasotec

C Lisinopril

D Benadryl

2. 250ml is equivalent to .... grams

A 121.5

B 131.5

C 141.7

D 151.7

3. All these are medical advantage plans except

A HMO

B PPO

C Fees for services

D PPI

4. The ....approves drugs for use in hospital setting

A Closed formulary

B Open Formulary

C Hospital drugs.

D P&T

5. Pharmacy technicians do not perform the following duty

A fill prescription

B insurance claims process

C clean the pharmacy shelves

D counsel patients

6. The device below is not a computer input device

A mouse

B keyboard

C scanner

D headphone

7 ………………is the brand name of Prilosec

A omeprazole

B pravachol

C flonase

D medrol

8. No medications selected, which DAW is used?

A 0

B 1

C 3

D 7

9. Amanda works in hospital and her DEA number is BA123648-. What is her last DEA number?

A 5

B 4

C 0

D 3

10. Which of the following requires patients package insert?

A Advil

B Isotretinoin

C Amoxicillin

D Acetaminophen

11 ……………..requires that all pharmacists perform drug utilization evaluation

A OBRA 90

B OBRA 87

C FDA

D NRC

12. All the following are enteral routes of administration except for which one?

A intravenous

B oral

C sublingual

D rectal

13. Which organization states 'Do not crush'?

A FDA

B OBRA

C JCHAO

D ISMP

14. How many bones are in the human body?

A 209

B 309

C 106

D 206

15. 1350 in Roman numerals

A MCCCL

B MCCLV

C MCVLC

D MCCCCL

16. Thrombolytic agents treat …………disease.

A cancer

B heart

C pain

D nervous

17. What form of substances require a material safety data sheet?

A needle syringe

B waste materials

C chemical/hazardous materials

D trash

18. Which type of communication is the most effective one?

A telephone

B face to face

C fax

D E-mail

19. A pharmacy technician certificate must be renewed every

A 12 months

B 6 months

C 72 months

D 24 months

20. A 14-year old boy weighs 110 pounds. He is prescribed to 5mg/kg of drug A daily. What will his dose be?

A 250mg

B 1200mg

C 1250mg

D 150mg

21. Which of the following is the brand name of Quetiapine

A Zovirax

B Clomid

C Seroquel

D Proscar

22. Albert went to Wal-Mart and informed the pharmacy technician that he wants a child resistant container for his medicine. Which law allows that?

A Poison Prevention Packaging Act

B Durham-Humphrey Amendment

C Food and Drug Administration

D Control Substances Act

23. Which of these capsule sizes has the greatest capacity?

A 0

B 1

C 2

D 3

24. A certification of pharmacy balance takes ……….

A 1 year

B 2 years

C 5 year

D 6 months

25. A patient has been prescribed 100mg of Tramadol, tablet available is 50mg. How many tablets will you give?

A 3

B 4

C 2

D 1

26. Which organization oversees MEDWATCH?

A ISMP

B KHA

C EPA

D FDA

27. All the following are enteral route except

A oral

B rectal

C sublingual

D intramuscular

28. CHF stands for ………

A chronic heart failure

B congestive heart failure

C chronic historian fee

D congestive histamine formula

29. Which of these is not a sign of incompatibility?

A change of color

B precipitation

C cloudiness

D shape

30. STATINS reconstituted products last for how many days?

A 7

B 8

C 10

D 9

31. What organization is responsible for form 222 of control substances sch.2?

A FDA

B HIPAA

C DEA

D CSA

32. Which of the following drugs is paired incorrectly?

A Clopidogrel – Plavix

B Spironolactone - Lasix

C Digoxin - Lanoxin

D Alprazolam – Xanax

33. A pharmacy shop was robbed of narcotic drugs. Which form would you use to report this?

A DEA 41

B DEA 106

C DEA 224

D DEA 222

34. The following are required for control substances prescription except

A beyond use date

B physician's DEA

C prescriber's address

D patient's address

35. Which container protects its content from air or gas?

A hermetic

B well closed

C single unit

D tight

36. ………………………is a sleep aid drug.

A Donepezil

B Alprazolam

C Digoxin

D Temazepam

37. How many millimeters are in 12 Ounces?

A 360

B 762

C 459

D 905

38. What is the sensitivity of a class A balance?

A 120mg

B 6mg

C 6kg

D 5kg

39. TJC certifies the following except

A nursing home

B hospital

C retail pharmacy

D long-term care facilities

40. A drug recall can be initiated by……….

A Hospital

B Patient

C Drug manufacturer

D Pharmacy

41. Which of the following pieces of information does an insurance company use to provide coverage authorization?

A authorization note

B proximity of the hospital

C DEA number

D identification number

42. Which of these is used in bipolar patients?

A lithium

B calcium

C fluoxetine

D vardenafil

43. All the following are automated counting devices used in community pharmacies except

A scriptPro

B baker cell

C robot-rx

D kirby-lester

44. In a retail pharmacy, a pharmacy 'B' transfers controlled substances [iii] to a pharmacy 'A' Which form is used to do this transfer?

A standard invoice

B transfer book

C DEA 222

D DEA 224

45. Which form is submitted every year by a retail pharmacy for destruction?

A DEA 106

B DEA 41

C DEA 222

D DEA 224

46. What do the last 2 numbers indicate in an NDC number?

A product

B manufacturer

C packaging

D logbook

47. What are benzodiazepines used for ....

A depression

B anxiety

C pain

D mental disorder

48. 1ml is equivalent to …….. drops

A 30

B 10

C 40

D 20

49. Which part of Medicare is responsible for doctor's appointment services?

A D

B C

C A

D B

50. Which of the following is the cost of pharmacy for medications?

A DDT

B GP

C AWP

D AAC

51. SSRI is for …………

A pain

B anxiety

C depression

D numbness

52. All of these are organizations found in health sectors except

A NATO

B FDA

C OBRA

D BOP

53. The suffix – olol refers to which drug class?

A H2 blockers

B calcium blockers

C beta blockers

D ar2 blockers

54. A patient has a written prescription which says 1 tab BID PO HS. Which of these below explains the exact information on the prescription?

A one tablespoon twice daily as needed for pain

B one tablet to be taken twice daily by mouth at bedtime

C one teaspoon to be taken twice daily as needed for pain

D one capsule to be taken twice by mouth at bedtime

55. How many milliliters are in 4 teaspoons?

A 10

B 50

C 20

D 40

56. Which of the following is the brain of a computer?

A monitor

B storage

C processor

D memory

57. Patients are responsible for

A co-pay and deductible

B billing their medications

C filling medications

D prescription of drug

58. Which of the following is the largest medical benefit established in 1965?

A Medicaid

B Tricare

C Medicare

D universal aid

59. Which organization oversees Medicare and Medicaid?

A CDC

B CMS

C State BOP

D FDA

60. Actual cost a pharmacy pays is equivalent to

A MAC + DISPENSING FEE

B AWP - AAC

C AAC + DISPENSING FEE

D ACC + DISPENSING FEE

61. Convert 225 Fahrenheit to degree Celsius

A 107

B 100

C 79

D 25

62. A patient brought a prescription to the pharmacy which had been altered. As pharmacy technician what would you do?

A inform the pharmacist

B dispense the drug

C give her time to come back

D let her know that the prescription is generic

63. What is the generic name for vitamin A?

A Retinol

B Clomid

C Bayer

D Alprazolam

64. A patient taking warfarin can't eat .....

A apple

B egg

C carrot

D spinach

65. Which medication is good for an allergy?

A Benadryl

B Seroquel

C Morphine

D Adderall

66. All the following are OTC drugs except

A Tylenol

B Benadryl

C Oxycontin

D Aspirin

67. What is the formula for calculating volume of intravenous solution if the time and the rate are given?

A multiply rate by time

B divide rate by time

C add rate and time

D subtract rate from time

68. In Clark's rule, weight of a child is measured in……

A ounces

B kilograms

C pounds

D pint

69. Patients who are 65 and above are called

A general

B pediatric

C geriatric

D old men

70. Aspirin is also known as……

A CMEA

B CSA

C BSA

D ASA

71. Which of these is not part of needle and syringe?

A lumen

B shaft

C tub

D plunger

72. Which of the following organizations is responsible for sterile compounding?

A CSA

B USP 795

C DEA 234

D USP 797

73. Which of these a pharmacy technician should not record in a compounding log?

A beyond use date

B lot numbers of ingredients

C name of medication

D address of the preparer

74. Drug shortage should be reported to

A CSA

B OSHA

C DEA

D FDA

75. A drug 'A' had serious consequences on 3 people who were rushed to and admitted at a hospital resulting in the death of one person. Which class of recall is that?

A class 1

B class 4

C class 2

D class 3

76. The following drugs are high-alert medications except

A opioids

B heparin

C Amoxicillin

D insulin

77. Which of the information is not required to be on a repackaging log?

A lot number

B beyond use date

C name of medication

D date of preparation

78. What drug can you substitute for Viagra?

A sildenafil

B tadalafil

C digoxin

D vardenafil

79. What is the sig code for every morning?

A qam

B pm

C ac

D pc

80. Take 1 tsp t.i.d prn pain. What does it mean?

A one teaspoon twice daily as needed for pain

B one tablespoon thrice daily as needed for pain

C one teaspoon thrice daily as needed for pain

D one tablespoon twice daily as needed for pain

81. A patient taking Aspirin cannot take ginseng due to …...

A food-drug interaction

B herbal-drug interaction

C drug-drug interaction

D drug-free interaction

82. What is the difference between reconstitution and trituration?

A reconstitution is a mixture of water and powder whilst trituration is a mixture of water and alcohol

B reconstitution is a suspension while trituration is a solution

C reconstitution is a combination of water and powder while trituration is a powder grind to form fine particles

D reconstitution is an iv solution while trituration is a solute

83. Why tall man lettering?

A to distinguish between tall letters

B to distinguish similarities between spelled drugs

C to show FDA labels

D to show similarities between proprietary drugs

84. A pharmacy technician has gone for a break, he/she returns after 15 minutes. What is the first thing he/she is supposed to do?

A wash her/his hands

B punch in

C fill prescription

D inform the pharmacist

85. Vicodin is under which drug classification?

A sch.1

B sch.2

C sch.3

D sch.4

86. Which law requires the phrase, "caution: federal law prohibits dispensing without a prescription"

A Durham-Humphrey Amendment

B Kefauver-Harris Amendment

C OBRA

D FDA

87. In Fred's rule, the age of the child is calculated in …

A years

B months

C days

D weeks

88. Which of the following pair is incorrect?

A Donepezil – Aricept

B Travoprost - Valtrex

C Buspirone – Buspar

D Ropinirole – Requip

89. A patient can't use the following drugs when driving except

A Valium

B Klonopin

C Ativan

D Tylenol

90. Which Medicare part is for Prescription drugs only?

A D

B C

C B

D A

91. Non sterile compounding is also known as…..

A permissive

B extemporaneous

C sterile

D community

92. Which of these below has two phases?

A suspension

B cream

C solution

D tablet

93. The Joint Commission certifies all the following except

A community pharmacy

B hospital pharmacy

C retail pharmacy

D nursing

94. Which organization may issue a drug recall?

A DHS

B HIPPA

C OSHA

D FDA

95. Which of the following has a patient package insert?

A Benadryl

B Tylenol

C Omeprazole

D Progesterone

96. Which of the following statements is not true?

A one tsp is equivalent to 5ml

B one tablespoon is equivalent to 15ml

C one pint is equivalent to 15ml

D one kilogram is equivalent to 1000gm

97. A pharmacy technician has been exposed to pathogens. He/she must submit her or his report to……?

A CDC

B CMC

C OSHA

D FDA

98. A sharp container is a container where used-syringes are kept. What is its color?

A white

B yellow

C blue

D red

99. A pharmacy technician has been instructed to fill prescription. In the process of filling this prescription, how many times would she view this?

A 3

B 4

C 5

D 6

100. Which information is not required on medication order label?

A lot number

B strength of drug

C address of the patient

D social security card

101. What pregnancy category has its benefits greater than its risks?

A X

B A

C D

D C

102. How many digits does NDC require for billing purposes?

A 11

B 10

C 9

D 8

103. A technique or procedure used to eliminate drug contamination with microbes/particles is called?

A eliminator

B consumer

C aseptic

D stocking

104. What kind of alcohol is recommended for cleaning laminar flow hood?

A 70% rubbing alcohol

B 70% isopropyl alcohol

C 70% alcoholic drink

D 70% alcohol

105. Which hood is used when preparing chemotherapeutic agents?

A vertical flow

B horizontal flow

C diagonal flow

D parallel flow

106. What should be added last when preparing TPN'S because of stability problems?

A sucrose

B amino acid

C fat

D dextrose

107. A drug X has an expiration date 04/18. What date below can the drug no longer be used?

A June 21, 2017

B December 30, 2017

C April 31, 2018

D May 20, 2018

108. Which organization is responsible for inspection of hospitals every 3 years?

A JCAHO

B NLC

C BOP

D HIPPA

109. Which drug suffix act as sedatives to treat seizure, sleep and anxiety disorders?

A -pam, -lam

B -olol, -nol

C -pril, - caine

D -artan, -dipine

110. The local anesthetics are designated by the …. Suffix

A pril

B caine

C olol

B artan

111. A solution contains 500mg/10ml. How many mg would be used to prepare 1 ounce of the solutions?

A 1000

B 1500

C 4507

D 2300

112. Doses can be expressed in the following ways except

A single

B daily

C total

D variety

113.A dose of 100mg is prescribed once daily for 7 days, calculate the single dose.

A 700mg

B 100mg

C 600mg

D 500mg

114. What is the dose for a 7-year old child who weighs 25 pounds If the adult dose is 450mg. Use Young's rule.

A 97.5

B 346.7

C 85.8

D 165.8

115. Which DAW code is used when a pharmacist has selected brand name even though substitution is allowed?

A 8

B 7

C 3

D 6

116. Which technology reduces medication errors?

A Nursing station

B Abbreviations

C USP 795

D Barcode Administration

117. All the following are schedule 4 drugs except?

A methadone

B alprazolam

C diazepam

D clonazepam

118. Which organization regulates the OTC sales of pseudoephedrine?

A CSA

B FDA

C DEA

D CMEA

119. Calculate the child's dose using the Clark's rule if the weight of the child is 35kg and the adult dose is 120mg.

A 61.6

B 67.1

C 41.6

D 47.1

120. The route of administration of drugs that involves the use of the veins.

A intradermal

B intravenous

C intramuscular

D subcutaneous

121. How many grams of Dextrose are needed for preparing 5% of 500ml solution?

A. 15g

B 55g

C 45g

D 25g

122. All the following are adverse effects of ACE inhibitors except

A dry cough

B stomach pain

C flu

D headache

123. Proton Pump Inhibitors reduce the production of ....in the stomach.

A base

B acid

C alkaline

D heartburn

124. Proton Pump Inhibitors should be taken before.............

A breakfast

B lunch

C evening

D night

125. Which of the following is meant to prevent and treat blood clots?

A Coumadin

B Lanoxin

C Nitropress

D Lasix

126. Aripiprazole is for Abilify, Olanzapine is for…………..

A Zyprexa

B Risperdal

C Lisinopril

D Paxil

127. Which of the following drugs is not antimigraine?

A Sumatriptan

B Zolmitriptan

C Ergotamine

D Dopamine

128. The sensitivity of counter balance is ………..

A 6mg

B 100mg

C 240kg

D 5kg

129 How many digits has a BIN number?

A 5

B 3

C 4

D 6

130. Which of the following medication is not on "Do not crush" list

A Vitamin C

B Prilosec

C Ms Contin

D Ambien

131. All the following are the reasons why some medications cannot be crushed except

A its slow-release nature

B its chewable nature

C its enteric-coated nature

D its taste

132. All the following are federal programs for patients older than 65 years except

A Medicaid

B Medicare

C Tricare

D Federal reserve

133. Which vitamin will increase the patient's blood when taking Coumadin?

A vitamin D

B vitamin C

C vitamin K

D vitamin B

134. What does CSA refer to?

A Control Substances Act

B Consumer Support Act

C Conference Schedule Art

D Control Substance Art

135. What is the maximum number of drugs that can be ordered on one form of DEA sh.2?

A 7

B 8

C 9

D 10

136. Which of the following drugs is a sch.2 drug?

A Tylenol

B Alprazolam

C Amoxicillin

D Methadone

137. What is the maximum number of refills allowed for sch.2 drug?

A 0

B 5

C 6

D 4

138. What type of inventory is done before the first day of business of the pharmacy?

A Initial

B biennial

C thrice

D perpetual

139. How many hours does a pharmacist need to complete the partial filling of a schedule 2 prescription?

A 24

B 48

C 72

D 96

140. How many digits has a package code of NDC?

A 4

B 5

C 2

D 3

141. A health benefits program for active duty service members and veterans is known as

A Care first

B Medicare

C Medicaid

D Tricare

142. At which phase can a pharmaceutical company request FDA approval for marketing its drug?

A Phase 1

B Phase 2

C Phase 3

D Phase 4

143. Which of the following is not a side effect of SSRI?

A Weight loss

B Nausea

C Diarrhea

D Dry mouth

144. In which class is the drug Meperidine?

A DEA Sch.5

B DEA Sch.4

C DEA Sch.3

D DEA Sch.2

145. What does the use of the Roman numeral "M" on prescription denote?

A 5000

B 1000

C 2000

D 100

146. If a doctor prescribes Penicillin 500mg b.i.d for 15 days how many 250mg capsules are needed to fill this medication?

A 20

B 40

C 60

D 50

147. How many grams of Sodium Chloride are in 100ml of Normal Saline solution?

A 0.9

B 0.09

C 0.009

D 9.00

148. You receive a prescription for Ibuprofen 200mg b.i.d. If you only have 400mg strength available, how many tablets should be dispensed for 3 days

A 200mg

B 600mg

C 300mg

D 1200mg

149. Which is not a basic unit of the metric system?

A grams

B liter

C grain

D volts

150. A doctor prescribed a medication for his patient and left the DAW blank, what was the doctor saying on the prescription?

A Generic version must be dispensed

B Brand must be dispensed twice

C Substitution is not allowed

D Brand drug mandated by law

151. What is teratogenic drug?

A Child deficit

B Embryo formulation

C Histamine drug

D Birth defect

152. What medication can you substitute for Orapred?

A Methadone

B Prednisolone

C Simvastatin

D Omeprazole

153. Rx: 1tab po bid qhs means

A One tablet by mouth twice daily at bedtime

B One tablespoon by mouth at bedtime

C One tab rectally per dose

D One tablet by mouth thrice daily as needed

154. Which drug among them is teratogenic drug?

A Tylenol

B Thalidomide

C Acetaminophen

D Benadryl

155. DUR report shows ....

A Prospective, concurrent and retrospective therapeutic evaluation

B Food and Administration officials

C DEA number and Anderson records

D Brand, generic and side effects of antihistamine drug

156. After using a syringe needle, a pharmacy technician should ....

A trash the needle in to a portable container

B dispose the needle into recapping device

C put the needle in to sharps container

D take the needle with gloves on

157. A child was playing with his or her parents Methadone without lock up cap, which organization is responsible for lock up cap?

A FDA

B Lock up cap companies

C PPPA

D CDC

158. A pharmacy technician should always wash her or his hands for ………

A 25 minutes

B 30 seconds

C 10 minutes

D 2 seconds

159. Which of the following is responsible for counseling patients?

A Pharmacy technician

B Licensed practical nurse

C Pharmacist

D Store manager

160. Amanda D went to hospital for check-up, what part of Medicare had been approved?

A B

B C

C D

D A

161. Which of these is the largest organ in the body?

A Eyes

B Skin

C Nose

D Tongue

162. A drug can be ordered and transferred from Pharmacy A to Pharmacy B for how many times?

A 4

B 3

C 2

D 1

163. What happens in class 1 HEPA filtering system?

A Filters exhaust air

B Filters hazardous materials

C Filters air until it becomes exhausted

D Filters air until it becomes less harmful

164. A doctor Thomas Snazzy DEA number BK 321456 was assigned to a controlled substance on original prescription. The prescription was pending and later rejected due to error in

A last name

B last DEA number

C last name and the DEA number

D Dispensing system

165. In Clinical trial research, which phase is based on collection of data on approved doses?

A 1

B 2

C 3

D 4

166. Which one is paired incorrectly?

A 1kg is equivalent to 20 drops

B 1kg is equivalent to 2.2 pounds

C 1kg is equivalent to 1000 grams

D 1kg is equivalent to 1000000 milligrams

167. A study of what happens to a drug when it is administered is known as

A Pharmacology

B Pharmacy

C Pharmacokinetics

D Pharmacodynamics

168. Which of the following is not sch.4 drug?

A Valium

B Warfarin

C Soma

D Ambien

169. Which of the following drugs is used for UTI?

A Glucotrol

B Pyridium

C Nitrostat

D Spiriva

170. All these routes of administration are enteral except for which one?

A Buccal

B Oral

C Sublingual

D Intramuscular

171. If one capsule contains 800mg, how many mg are in 5 capsules?

A 4000

B 10000

C 50000

D 100000

172. Using Fred's rule, calculate the child dose if the adult dose is 50mg and the age of the child is 11 months old.

A 2.7mg

B 6.5mg

C 3.7mg

D 4.6mg

173. Which of the following drugs is not restricted?

A Thalidomide

B Isotretinoin

C Clozapine

D Acetaminophen

174. Which organization makes "Do not use" list

A FDA

B ASHP

C USP

D TJC

175. The following information are required when dispensing controlled substances except

A Number of refill allowed

B The patient address

C Prescriber's address

D Beyond use date

176. The process whereby two insurance companies come together to pay claims for a client.

A Adjustable

B Adjudication

C Approvers

D Coordination of benefits

177. Which one best defines ScriptPro?

A An automated counting device that uses bar code to read prescription label to dispense.

B An automated counting device that receives prescription, picks exact drugs, count and does the packaging and labeling.

C An automated counting device that uses scanning and touch screen system.

D An automated counting device that uses bar codes reader to package medications

178. The word Brady means

A Slow

B Above

C Fast

D Under

179. Orphan drugs are developed specifically for……..diseases

A heart

B rare

C approved

D limited

180. A pharmacist instructed a technician to place the new drugs behind the old ones on the shelves. What term is the best for this instruction?

A Stock turnover

B Stock exchange

C Stock rotation

D Stock Replacement

181. To avoid medication error, which of the following is acceptable?

A 25.0mg

B .59mg

C .005mg

D 56mg

182. The first five digits of the NDC number represents

A Packaged product

B National drug expert

C Production

D Manufacturer

183. All the following drugs are teratogenic except

A Cocaine

B Thalidomide

C Isotretinoin

D Tylenol

184. Which form is used to destroy controlled substances?

A 224

B 222

C 106

D 41

185. Which medication below is classified as laxative?

A Timolol

B Lithium

C Docusate

D Oxcarbazepine

186. A patient was prescribed Warfarin 5mg PO once daily and later went to the nearest pharmacy to buy Aspirin. What kind of interaction is that?

A Food-drug

B Drug-drug

C Herbal-drug

D Herbal-food

187. Which of the following drugs needs regular blood test and follow up?

A Carbamazepine

B Benadryl

C Tylenol

D Tums

188. All the following drugs are calcium channel blockers except

A Amlodipine

B Verapamil

C Felodipine

D Famotidine

189. One pound is equivalent to ………

A 65mg

B 2pint

C 1ml

D 16oz

190. Warfarin is used to prevent all the following except

A Stroke

B Heart attack

C Blood clots

D Cholesterol

191. What is the w/w% of hydrocortisone if 30g of hydrocortisone is added to 300g of cold cream?

A 20%

B 10%

C 30%

D 40%

192. How long will 2.4 liters last if an IV solution is run at 150ml/hr?

A 16hrs

B 10hrs

C 14hrs

D 12hrs

193. A retail price of drug B $61.50 and a dispensing fee of $5.00. If the drug B has AAC of 41.50, what's its net profit?

A $40.00

B $20.00

C $10.00

D $15.00

194. A packet of Tylenol that regularly sells for $3.00 is marked down to $0.99, What is the discount rate?

A 100%

B 67%

C 60%

D 40%

195. What organization regulates OTC drugs for pseudoephedrine?

A FDA

B USP

C ASHP

D CMEA

196. Which of the following drugs is most potential for abuse and no medicinal value?

A Heroin

B Cocaine

C Vicodin

D Valium

197. All the following are measuring and weighing devices except

A Class A balance

B Counter balance

C Conical graduated cylinder

D Calculator

198. Which drug recalls has no adverse effect but violets FDA regulations?

A Class 3

B Class 1

C Class 2

D Class 4

199. MAR reports ……

A records of various treatments

B records of drug abuse

C legal records of drugs administered

D legal records of vaccines

200. Which of the following information is not on patient profile?

A Name of patient

B History of drug abuse

C Insurance information

D Drug manufacturer

201.First Tier drugs are generic name drugs that have the ……. co-pay

A highest

B lowest

C moderate

D slow

202. What happens in decentralized pharmacies?

A the pharmacist provides direct patient care

B the pharmacist negotiates with the patients

C the pharmacist is loaded with a lot of duties

D the pharmacist works with technicians

203. Which of these drugs can be classified as opiate?

A Tylenol

B Morphine

C Ranitidine

D Acetaminophen

204. A medication was given to a patient, in 5 minutes later he felt like vomiting. What might be the cause?

A side effect

B overdose

C drug-drug interaction

D herbal-drug interaction

205. Which of the following is the correct amount of change given to a customer after he bought Tylenol for $7.95 and paid $20.00?

A one ten dollar bill one quarter and one dime

B one ten dollar bill two one dollar bills and two nickels

C one ten dollar bill three one dollar bills and one dime

D one ten dollar bill two one dollar bills and one nickel

206. As a pharmacy technician what would you do if a drug container had no label?

A sell it to the customer

B inform the pharmacist

C place another label

D trash the drug

207. Why is it not advisable to recap a needle after use?

A it's dangerous, the needle could miss the cap and stab you

B because of sharps containers

C its dangerous because of coring

D its not necessary

208. Which of these is not the duty of pharmacy technicians?

A receiving and filing prescription

B acting like a pharmacist

C assisting in compounding

D assisting in billing process

209. All the following are narcotics except for

A Fentanyl

B Oxycontin

C Meperidine

D Colace

210. Calculate a child's dose if he is 6 years old and the adult dose is 80mg. Which formula below is the correct one to solve this problem?

A Clark

B Young

C Fred

D Proportions

211. FDA recalls a drug because it was mislabeled, under what class of recalls ?

A 1

B 2

C 3

D 4

212. Convert 456 Fahrenheit to Degree Celsius

A 235.6

B 322.6

C 323.6

D 352.6

213. Before administering a drug, there are many factors to review. Which of the following is not a factor to be reviewed?

A dosage and duration

B abuse

C drug-drug interaction

D prescription safety

214. Benzodiazepines are classified as

A Schedule 2 drugs

B Schedule 3 drugs

C Schedule 4 drugs

D Schedule 5 drugs

215. Flocculating agents are also called

A Electrolytes

B Aphrodite

C Narcotics

D Opiates

216. Captopril is a medication used for

A ulcer

B hypertension

C pain

D fever

217. One tablespoon is equivalent to

A 15ml

B 10ml

C 20ml

D 25ml

218. How many grams of active drug would contained in 300ml of a 1: 600 solution?

A 5

B 0.5

C 0.7

D 7

219. What is the percentage strength of a 1 : 300 solution?

A 0.1%

B 0.2%

C 0.3%

D 0.4%

220. What auxiliary label would you use for this prescription: ii gets AD bid?

A take with water

B for the ear

C for the eye

D take with milk

221. How many grams of dextrose is in 400ml of this solution if a 70% solution of dextrose is available?

A 480

B 380

C 280

D 180

222. Which of the following is available in patch?

A Lidocaine

B Acetaminophen

C Pepcid

D Tums

223. Amoxicillin oral suspension is stable in a refrigerator for ....days after reconstitution?

A 21

B 5

C 7

D 14

224. How much of each drug is needed if three drugs are combined to make a 2 : 3 : 5 of 120g ointment?

A 21, 36, 60

B 24, 36, 60

C 24, 36, 45

D 34, 63, 45

225. What is the best way of cleaning a laminar flow hood?

A front to back and top to down

B side to side and down to top

C back and down

D back to front and top to down

226. What size is a HEPA filter?

A 0.22 micron

B 0.33 micron

C 0.44 micron

D 0.55 micron

227. Ranitidine is also known as

A Seroquel

B Lisinopril

C Zantac

D Pepcid

228. Which of the following sets of vitamins are fat soluble?

A vitamin A, D, C and E

B vitamin A, D, E and K

C vitamin B, C, D and E

D vitamin B, D, E and K

229. What is the shelf-life of an antibiotic after reconstitution?

A 3/7 days

B 10/14 days

C 30/45 days

D 7/21 days

230. Terbutaline is classified as …………

A bronchodilator

B vasodilator

C angina

D bradycardia

231. What happens when a syringe is inserted incorrectly into a vial?

A the vial is broken

B the vial is stock

C it turns to be odd

D coring

232. Which term defines a drug being broken down by a liver?

A distribution

B elimination

C metabolism

D absorption

233. Amount of a drug prepackaged for a single administration is called

A unit dose

B single dosage

C multi dose

D self administration

234. Enteric-coated tablets are meant to dissolve in the…………….only

A cheek

B veins

C mouth

D intestines

235. Sublingual tablets are placed……………

A under the tongue

B under the skin

C between the cheek

D through the veins

236. How many numbers are there in a package size of National Drug Code?

A 1

B 2

C 3

D 4

237. Which of the following contains the highest concentration of alcohol?

A solution

B elixir

C tincture

D syrup

238. Graduated cylinders are more accurate than ……………

A flask

B balance A

C conical graduated

D HEPA filters

239. Buccal tablets are placed……………..

A under the tongue

B between the cheek and gum

C on the skin

D between the gum

240. All the following drugs are controlled substances except

A fentanyl

B tramadol

C morphine

D tums

241. Which of the following dissolves clot quickly?

A proton pump inhibitors

B ace inhibitors

C beta blockers

D thrombolytics

242. The hood should never be turned off. If it is off, then it must run for ………..

A 30 minutes

B 45 minutes

C 60 minutes

D 15 minutes

243. The HEPA filter in a vertical flow hood is located at ……..

A the back of the hood

B the front of the hood

C the top of the hood

D the side of the hood

244. All the following are electrolytes except

A magnesium

B gasoline

C sodium

D calcium

245. What's the sig code for 'every bedtime'

A hs

B ad

C ou

D qhs

246. If a prescription drug states: refill prn, for how long may this be refilled?

A 4 years

B 3 years

C 2 years

D 1 year

247. Which of the following medications can only be dispensed or stored in glass containers?

A Nitroglycerin iv form/sublingual

B Demerol

C Metoprolol

D Benadryl

248. Which of these drugs is therapeutic equivalent to Zestril?

A Prilosec

B Seroquel

C Lisinopril

D Ambien

249. How many grams of 2.5% hydrocortisone cream should be mixed with 30g of 1% hydrocortisone cream to make 1.5% hydrocortisone cream?

A 10

B 20

C 30

D 40

250. Which of the following drugs is not a controlled substance?

A Adderall

B Lidocaine

C Oxycontin

D Amoxicillin

251. Which formula would you use to convert Fahrenheit to Degree Celsius?

A c = 5f - 160

B c = 5f – 160 divided by 9

C f = 9c + 160

D f = 9c + 160 divided by 5

252. Glucocorticoids fight against ....

A inflammation

B viruses

C blood clot

D chest pain

Use the table below to answer questions 253 and 255

Number of capsules	Size of capsules
1	000
2	00
3	0
4	1
5	2
6	3
7	4
8	5

253. Which number has the smallest size of capsule?

A 8

B 1

C 3

D 7

254. Which number has the largest size of capsule?

A 5

B 4

C 8

D 1

255. How many size of capsules are there in the table?

A 4

B 7

C 8

D 9

256. Which of these reduces muscle spasm in the intestines?

A angina

B bronchodilator

C vasodilator

D anticholinergic

Use the diagram below to answer questions 257 - 260

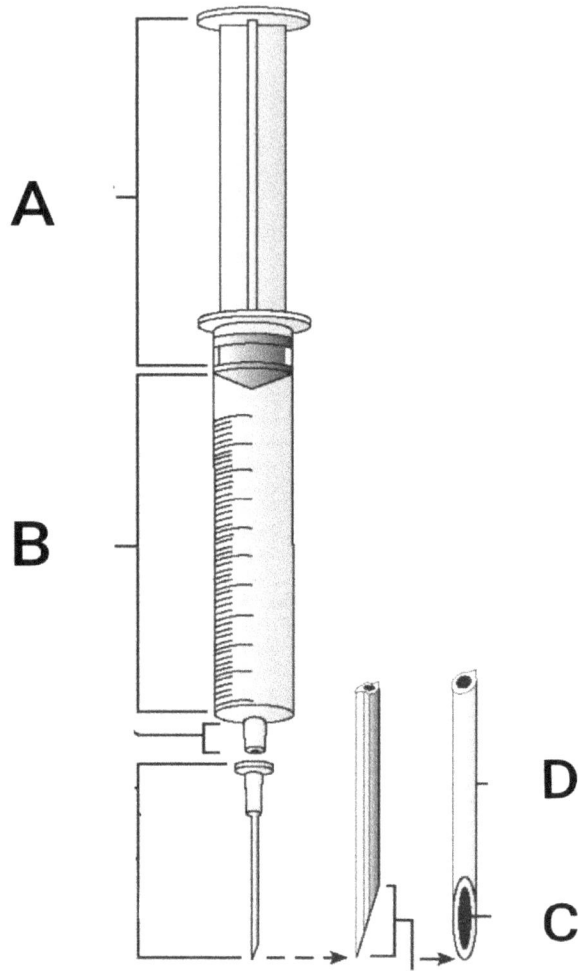

257. Which part of the syringe needle labeled 'A'?

A shaft

B plunger

C barrel

D lumen

258. Which part of the syringe needle is called lumen?

A B

B D

C A

D C

259. Which part is labeled 'D'?

A bevel

B shaft

C tip

D plunger

260. Which part of the syringe needle holds the content of the medication?

A barrel

B plunger

C hub

D lumen

261. How much of 80% alcohol must be mixed with 20% alcohol to make 473ml of a 30% alcohol solution?

A 34.7

B 78.8

C 65.6

D 93.8

262. What term defines low blood glucose level?

A hyperglycemia

B hypoglycemia

C hypotension

D hypertension

263. A mixture of two or more ingredients for enteral route of administration use is known as………..

A suspension

B punch method

C sterile compounding

D extemporaneous

Use the table below to answer questions 264 – 268

Drug	Cost	Markup	Selling Price	% Markup
A	$21.00	$13.50	%34.50	------
B	-------	$27.00	$72.57	59.2%
C	$69.00	--------	$78.00	13%
D	$50.00	$77.00	--------	154%
E	-----------	$45.00	$128.67	53.8%

264. What is the percentage markup for drug 'A'?

A 64.3%

B 59.2%

C 53.8%

D 145%

265. Find the cost price of drug 'E'

A $83.67

B $67.43

C $50.00

D $34.67

266. Calculate the markup price of drug 'C'

A $16.56

B $65.00

C $23.43

D $9.00

267. Find the selling price of drug 'D'

A $80.00

B $19.00

C $127.00

D $64.97

268. Which drug has the highest percentage markup?

A B

B D

C A

D C

269. Which statement is not true?

A whole number should always have a trailing zero

B make your decimal points more visible

C decimal point should never be left alone

D never use a whole number with a decimal point and a trailing zero

270. Which of these drugs can be taken in the morning before breakfast for acid reflux?

A Adderall

B Acetaminophen

C Morphine

D Prilosec

271. All the following are sig codes used for eye medication except

A ad

B os

C od

D ou

272. A patient brought a prescription to the pharmacy. It was written on the prescription 'PRN'. What does PRN stand for?

A as needed

B pure refilled nitrogen

C in 15 minutes time

D as soon as possible

ANSWERS

1..C, Lisinopril is a brand name for Zestril

2...A, 121.5gm is equal to 250ml

3...D, PPI is not a medical advantage plan

4.. D, The P&T approves drugs for use in hospital setting

5....D, Pharmacy technicians do not counsel patients

6...D, Headphone is an output device

7....A, Omeprazole is the brand name of Prilosec

8...A, DAW code O is used when no medication is selected

9...A, 5 is the last DEA number

10..B, Isotretinoin requires patients package insert.

11..A, OBRA 90 requires that all pharmacists perform drug utilization evaluation

12..A, Intravenous is an enteral route of Administration

13..D, ISMP states "Do not crush"

14....D, 206 bones in human body

15...A, MCCL is 1350 in Roman numerals

16...B, Thrombolytic agents treat heart disease

17...C, Chemical/hazardous materials requires MSDS

18...B, Face-to-face is the most effective communication

19...D, 24 months (2 years) is the renewal duration for Pharmacy technician

20...A, 250mg

21...C, Seroquel is the brand name of Quetiapine

22...A, Poison Prevention Packaging Act

23...A, 'O' has the greatest capacity

24...A, Certification of pharmacy balance takes 1 year

25...C, 2

26...D, FDA oversees MEDWATCH

27...D, Intramuscular is a parenteral route of administration

28...B, Congestive Heart Failure

29...D, Shape is not a sign of incompatibility

30...C, STATINS reconstitute products last for 10 days

31..C, DEA is responsible for form 222 of control substances sch.2

32...B, Spironolactone is paired incorrectly to Lasix

33...B, DEA 106 form is used for theft or loss cases

34...A, Beyond use date is not required for controlled substances prescription

35...A, Hermetic container protects its content from air or gas

36...D, Temazepam is a sleep aid drug

37..A, 360ml is equivalent to 12 ounces

38...B, 6mg is the sensitivity of a class A balance

39...C, TJC does not certify a retail pharmacy

40...C, Drug manufacturers can initiate drug recall

41...D, An insurance company uses identification number to provide information

42..A, Lithium is used in bipolar patients

43...C, Robot-rx is not a device used in community pharmacy

44...A, Standard invoice is used to order drugs for sch.3, 4 and 5 substances

45...B, DEA 41 is a form use for destruction of Control substances

46...C, Packaging is the last 2 numbers indicate in an NDC numbers

47...B, Benzo is an anxiety drug

48...D, 20 drops equal to 1ml

49...D, Medicare B is responsible for doctor's appointment services

50...D, AAC is the actual cost of pharmacy for medications

51...C, SSRI is for depression

52...A, NATO is not an organization in health sectors

53...C, The suffix -olol refers to Beta blockers

54...B, One tablet to be taken twice daily by mouth at bedtime

55...C, 20ml is equivalent to 4 teaspoons

56...C, The processor is the brain of a computer

57...A, Patients are responsible for co-pay and deductible

58...C, Medicare is the largest medical benefit established in America in 1965

59...B, CMS is an organization that oversees Medicare and Medicaid

60...C, AAC + DISPENSING FEE is the actual cost pharmacy paid

61...A, 107, using the formula: 5f = 9c + 160

62...A, inform the pharmacist

63...A, Retinol is the generic name for Vitamin A

64...D, Spinach (food-drug interaction)

65....A, Benadryl is an allergic medication

66....C, Oxycontin is a sch.2 controlled substance

67....A, Volume = rate × time

68....C, Weight of a child is measured in pounds by using Clark's rule

69....C, Geriatric

70....D, Aspirin is also known as ASA

71....C, Tub is not part of needle syringe

72....D, USP 797 is responsible for sterile compounding

73....D, Address of the preparer is not recorded on compounding log

74...D, Drug shortage must be reported to FDA

75...A, Class 1

76...C, Amoxicillin is not high alert medication

77....D, Date of preparation is not required on repackaging log

78...A, Sildenafil

79...A, qam means every morning

80...C, One teaspoon thrice daily as needed for pain

81...B, Herbal-drug interaction

82...C, Reconstitution is a combination of water and powder while trituration is a powder grind to form fine particles

83....B, Tall man letters are used to distinguish similarities between spelled drugs

84....A, Wash her/his hands

85....B, Vicodin is sch.2 drug classification

86....A, Durham-Humphrey Amendment ensures "CAUTION": federal law prohibits dispensing without a prescription" label written on package of prescription drugs.

87....B, Months

88....B, Travoprost is paired incorrectly to Valtrex

89....D, Tylenol

90....A, Medicare part D

91....B, Non sterile compounding is also known as Extemporaneous

92....A, Suspension has 2 phases

93....C, The Joint Commission does not certify retail pharmacies

94....D, FDA may issue a drug recall

95....D, Progesterone has a patient package insert

96....C, One pint is not equivalent to 15ml

97....A, CDC

98...D, The color of a sharp container is red

99....A, 3 times

100...D, Social security card

101....D, C has its benefit greater than its risk in pregnancy category

102....A, 11 digits of NDC for billing

103....C, Aseptic is a technique used to eliminate drug contamination with microbes/particles

104....B, 70% isopropyl alcohol

105.....A, Vertical flow hood is used when preparing of chemotherapeutic agents

106.....B, Amino acid is added last when preparing TPN'S because of stability problems

107.....C, April 31, 2018

108.....A, JCAHO is responsible for hospital inspection

109.....A, -pam, -lam are suffix

110.....B, - caine is a suffix for local anesthetic

111.....B, 1500mg

112.....D, Doses cannot be expressed in variety

113......B, 100mg

114......D, 165.8

115......C, DAW 3

116......D, Barcode Administration reduces medication errors

117......A, Methadone is not sch.4 drug

118......D, CMEA regulates OTC sales of pseudoephedrine

119......A, 61.6

120.......B, Intravenous

121........D, 25gm

122.......B, Stomach pain

123.......B, Acid

124.......A, Proton Pump Inhibitors should be taken before breakfast

125......A, Coumadin prevents and treats blood clots

126.......A, Zyprexa

127.......D, Dopamine is not antimigraine drug

128.......B, 100mg is the sensitivity of counter balance

129.......D, BIN number has 6 digits

130.......A, Vitamin C

131.......B, Its chewable nature

132.......A, Federal reserve

133.......C, Vitamin K

134.......A, Controlled Substances Act

135.......D, 10 drugs can be ordered on one form of DEA sch 2.

136.......D, Methadone is a sch.2 drug

137.......A, Zero refill for sch.2 drugs

138.....A, Initial inventory is done

139......C, Partial filling of sch.2 prescription takes 72 hours to complete.

140......C, A package code has 2 digits number.

141.....B, Tricare is a health benefits program for active duty service members and veterans.

142.....C, A pharmaceutical company can request FDA approval for marketing its drug after completing phase 3 clinical trial.

143....A, Weight loss

144....D, DEA Sch.2

145 ...B, M represents 1000

146 ...C, 60

147 ...A, 0.9

148 ....D, 1200mg

149 ....D, Kilometer is not a basic unit of the metric system

150 ....A, Generic version must be dispensed

151 ....D, Teratogenic drugs are drugs that cause birth defect in pregnant women

152 ....B, prednisolone

153 ....A, One tablet by mouth twice daily at home

154 ....B, Thalidomide is teratogenic

155 ....A, Prospective, concurrent, retrospective therapeutic evaluation

156. ...C, Place the used needle in sharps container

157 ....C, PPPA

158 ...B, 30 seconds

159 ....C, Pharmacist

160 ...A

161 ..B, Skin

162 ..D, One time

163 ...C, Filters air until it becomes exhausted

164 ...C, Last name and the DEA number

165 ...A, 1

166 ...A, 1kg is not equivalent to 20 drops

167 ..C, Pharmacokinetics

168 ..B, Warfarin

169 ..B, Pyridium

170 ..D, Intramuscular

171 ..A, 4000

172 ...C, 3.7mg

173 ...D, Acetaminophen

174 ...D, TJC

175 ...D, beyond use date

176 ...D, Coordination of benefits

177 ...B, An automated counting device that receives prescription, picks exact drugs, count and does the packaging and labeling

178 ....A, Brady means slow

179 ...B, Orphan drugs are developed specifically for rare diseases

180 ...C, Stock rotation

181 ....D, 56mg

182 ....D, Manufacturer

183 ...D, Tylenol is not teratogenic

184 ...D, 41

185 ..C, Docusate

186 ...B, Drug-drug interaction

187 ...A, Carbamazepine

188 ...D, Famotidine

189 ...D, 16oz

190 ...D, Cholesterol

191 ...B, 10%

192 ...A, 16hrs

193 ...D, $15.00

194 ...B, 67%

195 ...D, CMEA

196 ...A, Heroin

197 ...D, Calculator

198 ...A, Class 3

199 ...C, Legal records of drugs administered

200 ..D, Drug manufacturer

201 ..B, First tier drugs are generic name drugs that have the lowest co-pay

202...A, The pharmacist provides direct patient care

203...B, Morphine

204...A, Side effect

205...D, One ten dollar bill two one dollar bills and one nickel

206...B, Inform the pharmacist

207...A, It's dangerous, the needle could miss the cap and stab you

208...B, Acting like a pharmacist

209...D, Colace

210...B, Young

211...C, 3

212...A, 235.6

213...D, Prescription safety

214...C, Schedule 4 drugs

215...A, Electrolytes

216...B, Hypertension

217..A, 15ml

218...B, 0.5

219...C, 0.3%

220...B, For the ear

221...C, 280

222...A, Lidocaine

223...D, 14

224...B, 24, 36, 60

225...D, Back to front and top to down

226...A, 0.22 micron

227...C, Zantac

228...B, Vitamin A, D, E, and K

229...B, 10/14 days

230...A, Bronchodilator

231...D, Coring

232...C, Metabolism

233...A, Unit dose

234...D, Intestines

235...A, Under the tongue

236...B, 2

237....C, Tincture

238....C, Conical graduated

239....B, Between the cheek and gum

240....D, Tums

241....D, Thrombolytics

242....A, 30 minutes

243....C, The top of the hood

244....B, Gasoline

245....D, qhs

246....D, 1 year

247....A, Nitroglycerin iv form/sublingual

248....C, Lisinopril

249....A, 10

250....D, Amoxicillin

251....B, 5f - 160 divided by 9

252....A, Inflammation

253...A, 8

254...D, 1

255...C, 8

256...D, Anticholinergic

257...B, Plunger

258...D

259...B, Shaft

260...A, Barrel

261...B, 78.8

262...B, Hypoglycemia

263...D, Extemporaneous

264...A, 64.3%

265...A, $83.67

266...D, $9.00

267...C, $127.00

268...B

269...A, Whole number should always have a trailing zero

270...D, Prilosec

271...A, ad

272...A, As needed

www.ingramcontent.com/pod-product-compliance
Lightning Source LLC
Chambersburg PA
CBHW081154270326
41930CB00014B/3152